# Stop and
# Sell the Roses

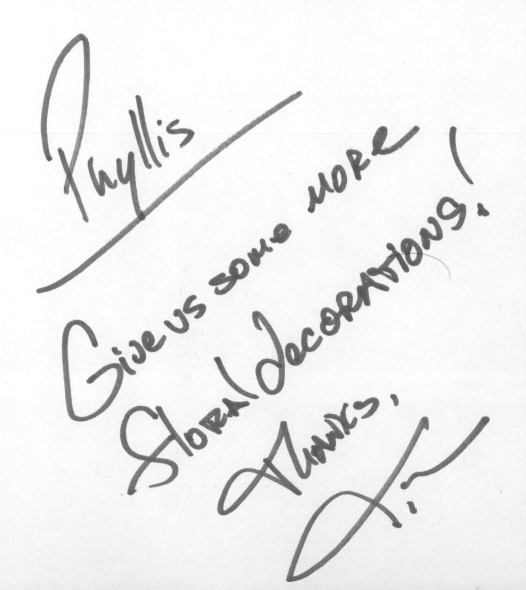

Phyllis

Give us some more
floral decorations!

Thanks,

# Stop and
# Sell the Roses

## Lessons from
## Business & Life

# JIM McCANN

### with Peter Kaminsky

BALLANTINE BOOKS • NEW YORK

A Ballantine Book
Published by The Ballantine Publishing Group

Copyright © 1998 by Jim McCann

http://www.randomhouse.com

LIBRARY OF CONGRESS CATALOGING-IN-PUBLICATION DATA
McCann, Jim, 1951–
Stop and sell the roses: lessons from business & life / Jim McCann with
Peter Kaminsky. — 1st ed.
p.     cm.
ISBN 0-345-41675-9 (alk. paper)
1. Florists—New York (State)—New York.   2. Flowers—New York (State)—
New York—Marketing.   3. McCann, Jim, 1951–      .   4. 1-800-FLOWERS
(Firm)   I. Kaminsky, Peter.   II. Title.
SB443.35.N7M33   1998
745.92'068—DC21                                                    97-46399
                                                                         CIP

Designed by Holly Johnson

Manufactured in the United States of America

First Edition: May 1998

10   9   8   7   6   5   4   3   2   1

*To my father, for giving me his work ethic and drive*
*To my mother, for teaching me the importance of compassion*
*To my wife, Marylou, for making the tough times easier and the
good times better*

# Contents

CONTENTS

# Acknowledgments

Writing a book is never easy, and it's particularly challenging if you're supposed to be running a company at the same time. This project could never have been completed without the assistance and support of many people, starting with my family: Marylou; my children, Erin, Jim, and Matthew; and my brothers and sisters: Julie, who does a great job as our consumer spokesperson and is one of the most creative, energetic people I know, and Peggy and Kevin, who have worked side by side in the floral business with Julie, my brother Chris, and me.

A special thanks goes to Chris, 1-800-FLOWERS' senior vice president. Chris runs the operations side of our business and does it better than anyone I know. He'd be the top guy at any other company, and I feel fortunate to have him backing me up and keeping me (and our company) on track.

Another person I must mention is my friend Larry Zarin. I've had the pleasure of working with Larry, off and on, for several years. He's a talented, creative guy who has contributed to the success of 1-800-FLOWERS and, in particular, to the thoughts developed in this book.

There are a number of "core" people I also want to mention here. These are the people who have been with us for several years and who I fully expect to be with us for many more. These talented people include Jerry Gallagher, Tom Hartnett, Donna Iucolano, Glenn Reed, and Bill Shea.

I also want to acknowledge the support of the entire 1-800-FLOWERS team, whose hard work and support enabled me to take the time to tackle this project; my assistant, Patty Altadonna, who does the impossible every day by keeping me organized and focused; and Ken Young, who helped quarterback this project for the last year and a half.

Thanks also to Peter Kaminsky, my collaborator on this book and one talented dude; Mark Reiter, my agent at IMG; and Judith Curr, Cathy Repetti, and the entire Ballantine team.

Thank you to all 1-800-FLOWERS' customers, my friends, and my business associates who, directly or indirectly, have contributed to this project. I couldn't have done it without you.

Finally, I want to thank my late parents for providing the foundation for whatever success I've achieved to date. Although they had contrasting styles—my father was the taskmaster and my mother was, well, my mother—they each taught me valuable lessons, many of which are expressed in this book. Mom, Dad, I think about you every day. This one's for you.

# Introduction

## I SAW IT ON THE RADIO

I'm riding along the Meadowbrook Parkway. It's a hot August evening. The air is sticky and still. It has just rained, and a sweet steam, full of the salty smell of Jones Beach, a few miles south, rises off the asphalt. I swear I can smell suntan lotion on the wind. Every so often, as I look off to the west, I can see the Twin Towers. Sam and Dave are blasting on the oldies station. I flick on the news looking for a Mets score. It was a day game. Maybe their bullpen didn't fall apart today.

First the traffic with the usual grim report: a two-mile backup. There's a five-car accident coming off the Whitestone Bridge. AccuWeather promises more heat and humidity. Next, the local news:

". . . Father John O'Mahoney, a visiting Irish priest on his first trip to New York, was mugged today on the A train in Rockaway. He was accosted by three youths as the train pulled into the 105th Street Station shortly after 1:30 this morning. According to police, the suspects approached O'Mahoney and demanded his wallet, which he handed over with no argument. When it turned out to hold no more than fifteen dollars, the enraged ringleader of the gang slashed the priest with a broken bottle, opening a wound that required multiple stitches. Late this morning the suspects were apprehended at their residence, a home for boys in Rockaway Beach."

I sat straight up as if someone had poured a bucket of ice water on me. *A home for boys in Rockaway!!?* There was only one, the St. John's Home for Boys. All of a sudden a feeling washed over me and the years melted away. My snazzy Porsche became the rickety Ford Falcon that I drove to work all those years ago when I was broker than broke, redlined on my credit cards. The street-scarred kids from way back then rose up before me. I could see them all shaking their heads at the three dumb-ass kids who had no more brains than to roll a poor priest. First I saw Tony, a bit slow-witted but weightlifter strong. Then Norman, with his flashy clothes and a secret knack with tomatoes; and Ernie and Bill—the enforcers who from time to time worked their intimidatingly persuasive magic on Joe, who would threaten to kill anyone who mussed his every-hair-in-place do. They were supposed to be my students. But they were also my teachers. We learned from each other.

## Chapter One

# The Original Honeymooners

Every life has a turning point. Mine happened in a vacant lot in Richmond Hill. Until then, I was an undirected long haired kid with a major in psychology that, I thought, qualified me to drive a cab or tend bar. As a Queens Irish male, I felt it part of my genetic heritage that I put in at least a few years as a bartender. So I poured shots and beers for the cops and firemen, telephone company guys, and Con Edison workers who made up most of the working population in Richmond Hill. It was a real Honeymooners neighborhood where Ralph Kramden and Alice would have fit right in. I am quite sure that in the sixty-odd years that my grandparents (and then my parents) ran our family's small painting business, no one in Richmond Hill ever used the word "entrepreneur." I certainly never heard it and, if I had, it wouldn't have sounded like something I wanted to be.

So there I was drinking beer, playing cards, hanging out with my friends, putting in time but not doing very much with it. One of the regulars at the bar was a guy named Bob Farrell. He used to come in after working at this home for teenage boys, after which he was more than ready for a drink. We used to get to talking about the troubled backgrounds these kids came from and the tremendous odds against them in life. It was interesting to me.

One afternoon, Farrell came in and said, "McCann, you seem so interested in the work out at the group home, maybe you should come out and have a look. You can always come back and tend bar." I figured, why not? The next morning Bob and I played nine holes of golf at the city course at Forest Park. Then we drove out to Richmond Hill, to a two-story brick house that looked out on a serious inner-city housing project. We went inside and met a couple of the boys. By way of making conversation, I told Bob it looked like a really neat place.

"Glad you like it," Bob said as he threw me the keys to the front door. "You're on duty tonight!"

And that's how I began a fourteen-year relationship with the home for boys run by the Marianist Brothers, a mendicant order all of whose members had taken a vow of poverty and spent their lives helping the poor and teaching. These kids weren't like me. My family may not have had a lot of money, but we weren't poor folks. We held jobs, paid taxes, and, for the most part, stayed out of jail. These boys were New York kids in trouble, kicked out of homes that didn't want them, by mothers who could no longer cope or just plain didn't care. The lucky ones never knew their dads; the others had tales of abuse and fathers in prison. Although that world was alien to me, something about the work struck me as interesting. I was drawn to it. It was a challenge to try and reach these kids and help them get their lives on track when every other thing in their environment was pushing them the other way.

I was the night guy at the home. I came on duty at four in the afternoon, got the boys fed with the help of the house mother, into bed, and, at least in theory, on their way to school in the morning. Corralling a bunch of reform school refugees was probably safer than fighting the Vietcong, but I would say I had an equal chance of swaying both groups on personality and charm.

I was clueless. Worse, I was smaller than some of the boys. Not only was I in fear for my life, I was getting the square root of zero accomplished with the kids. I'd sit on the couch watching TV. If a fight broke out, I tried to break it up. If someone skipped school that day, I'd ask why and tell him he really should go to school. I was, in the street talk of those years, "The Man," but I was perceived more as Barney Fife than Kojak.

# BROTHER TOM'S BETTING METHOD

"Brother Tom," I said to the young brother who had hired me, "I'm no good at this. I think I'm going to move on."

Brother Tom had come to his work as the head of the Marianist Brothers after years as a high school disciplinarian, where he had earned a reputation for strictness tempered by wisdom and compassion. He could smell defeat and resignation oozing out of me, two qualities that tried his patience. "You're not doing much good because you are just reacting," he said.

"Well, what do you do?" I asked.

"I try to find a way to engage the kids, get them interested, establish contact."

I didn't know it then, but Brother Tom had just spoken the words that would change my life.

"What would you say if I told you that I got Radenus Lopez to read Vachel Lindsay?" he asked.

It seemed unlikely that Radenus, whose taste ran more to Parliament Funkadelic, would have found much in the musings of a regular old American poet, but Brother Tom had that winding-up-to-make-a-point look that I had come to recognize.

"Not the Lindsay type," I answered.

"If I asked him right now, he could walk in here and recite all of 'Factory Windows Are Always Broken.' And José Gonzalez is good for most of Edward Arlington Robinson's 'Richard Corey.' And Tony Vidale, he's my prize: how about all but the last two verses of Robert Browning's 'Pied Piper of Hamelin.' "

"Brother Tom, I'd say either you're delusional or you're setting me up for a lecture about the power of prayer."

"Come on, McCann, everything in its place. I know who I am dealing with. Prayer might help with their souls, but not memorizing poetry. No, I bet them."

"How do you mean?"

"I mean I tell them I will pay $5 for Lindsay, start to finish without a mistake. Robinson pays $20, and Browning, which no one ever gets, goes for $250."

"Sounds like a lot."

"Actually, I don't have to pay more than a few kids a year but it's well worth it. Two or three times a week one of them comes up to me and tells me he is ready. And they have to get it all out on the first try, no mistakes. They really want the money. In the meantime, I have accomplished a few things. One: the kids, even if they don't win the bet, all learn a little bit of great poetry. Two, they've found that learning isn't always painful. In fact, it can be fun. Three, and most important, we've made contact, we're talking to each other, getting to know each other, establishing a relationship."

Brother Tom's point was obvious, but it hit home with tremendous clarity. Establish a relationship, make contact, and then everything else is possible.

"And one other thing," Brother Tom added, "stop being the one who has to react all the time. You need to come with a plan. Not for the rest of your life, but for the day."

## A TOMATO AT LIFE'S CROSSROADS

I needed a plan, Brother Tom said. That sounded easy enough, but you'd be surprised how the self-help section at the bookstore has very few books in the section titled "How to Motivate Juvenile Delinquents to Clean Their Rooms,

Say Their Prayers, and Make Their Beds." I left Brother Tom thinking two things about his advice. First, it sounded like good advice. And second, I still didn't know where to begin. Next day, before work, I stopped off to see my mom, who was of the opinion that God created backyards so that she could raise tomato plants. My mom loved those big gnarly beef-steak tomatoes that taste like they've somehow captured all the sunshine of July.

When I arrived at my folks', I saw that Mom had fully crammed a little section of our yard with her plants. Like all moms who raise tomatoes, she had bought many more plants than she could ever hope to use. An idea struck me. Maybe "idea" is too intellectual a word for what I had. Call it an instinct.

"Mom, do you mind if I take those extra plants to work with me?"

My mother beamed with maternal joy. There was still hope for me! When I got to the home, I began to dig up the ground in the scraggly little patch next to the parking lot. This caught the attention of Norman, one of the tougher-to-reach kids in the home (you had to be tough to survive in Crown Heights with a name like Norman). His family life, like that of a lot of kids at the home, had been disastrous. Norman was five-foot-nine—in all directions— and he pumped iron whenever he had nothing better to do, which was all the time.

Norman watched me tilling the dirt and immediately knew that something was up. In that part of the world, when a guy pulled up to an empty patch of ground, pulled a shovel from the trunk of his car, and started digging, the question that would naturally occur to the observant passerby was not "what" but "who" was he planting.

"Mister Jim, what are you doing there?" he asked, addressing me in the old-fashioned way that all the kids talked to me.

"Planting tomatoes," I answered.

Norman thought this was either the funniest or the stupidest thing he had heard in a long time—maybe both.

"Mister Jim, I thought you were planting something useful, like pot. I give those ratty little tomato plants about twenty minutes in the ground before somebody comes along and rips them up," he counseled in the tones of someone wise in the ways of the Big City.

I disagreed, but it didn't matter. I had produced a reaction in the normally unreachable Norman. We were actually talking to each other. This was a tremendous step forward for me, which shows you how miserably I was doing in my job up to that point. After a few minutes, Norman, the mean streets realist, picked up a stake and handed it to me. He asked if it would be all right if he planted one of the tomatoes. I made like it was a big deal for me to let him handle my precious plants.

We planted two whole rows, staked them, watered them, and stood back to admire them. Next day, when I got to work, Norman was there to help me water and pull weeds. And the next day, and the next. We talked about sports, girls, school, whatever was going on in Norman's life. It didn't matter to me what we talked about as long as we kept talking.

The tomatoes were beside the point. We could have

been playing electric guitars, trading *Playboy* magazines, or counting Chevrolet pickup trucks as they passed by. The important thing was that we had something in common. With that bond established, Norman was receptive to what I was selling, or at least he was willing to hear my pitch.

Just as Brother Tom advised, I had made contact, formed a relationship. From that first tomato plant, there emerged the philosophy upon which we built 1-800-FLOWERS. If there is just one commandment for success in business, certainly in any retail business, it is this: *First make a relationship, then do business.* It's the simplest piece of advice I can give you, but the most valuable. Give the other guy the feeling "This person cares about my problems, cares about me." You'll make more than a sale. You'll have a steady customer.

The relationship *is* the transaction. The exchange of money and goods is just the external sign. Technology can extend your reach and multiply your contacts, but you still have to make contact. I had to reach those kids in Queens. 1-800-FLOWERS has to reach our customers across the phone and the internet. The task is the same: reaching people and establishing a bond. Fun is one way to establish a bond. Service is another. But the bond is the thing that makes everything else happen.

## FRENCH CRULLERS AND THE POWER OF PRAYER

The first time I understood the power of that bond was with Dave the milkman, back in Ozone Park. Dave never went to business school. In fact, I wouldn't swear that Dave finished high school. But he knew about building a relationship as the foundation of a business. Dave was a home delivery guy in the days when the milkman and the fruit and vegetable guy still came to your door. He knew the latest news about everybody in the neighborhood. Like Santa Claus, he knew if we kids had been naughty or nice and, although usually he could be counted on not to rat on us, if we ever stepped seriously out of line, Dave let our folks know about it.

My dad ran our small painting contracting business out of our grandmother's house. Every morning, my dad and my uncles and a couple of the workmen would be there having coffee. My grandmother would make three big pots of it in the days before electric coffeemakers. Sometimes Grandma Margaret would forget that the percolator was on; it would boil over and the grounds would burn on the stove top. That coffee of hers was strong enough to peel paint (I know—I tried it). While the men talked about sports, they ate crusty hard rolls from Carver's Bakery. We spread thick pats of Sealtest butter and gobs of strawberry jam on the rolls.

Dave was the delivery guy for Sealtest. (Sealtest was a local dairy that I remember as a sponsor on *The Ed Sullivan Show*, which at the time made me very proud and somehow closer to show business.) Every morning he'd pull up to the driveway, push in the screen door with his shoulder, and enter talking about the weather and the Yankees (until I was ten, I thought rooting for the Yankees was part of the Nicene Creed). He would tell us about Mrs. Gillespie's strained back and how the Murphy brothers were caught selling firecrackers behind Our Lady of Perpetual Help. While Dave talked, my grandmother looked through his tray and picked milk, cottage cheese, buttermilk, and maybe—if we were lucky—something sweet from Dave's bakery tray.

Dave carried the most sugary, puffiest French crullers I had ever tasted. Whenever Grandma went to the tray, I would pray as hard as I ever prayed for anything, "Please, please go for the French crullers!" Sometimes she picked them and sometimes she didn't. We couldn't always afford them, which made the times we could that much more special. I couldn't wait for Dave to arrive in the morning. I would often wait for him on the stoop. We had a relationship. Because of that personal relationship with Dave, we had a personal relationship with his brand. All the positive aspects of our feelings for Dave carried over into loyalty to his product. As Dave taught me, a relationship with a brand often grows from a relationship with the people who sell that brand. Years later, when I went in hock for seven million dollars to acquire the right to use a phone number, I realized that if I were going to make a going business out of something that impersonal, I would have to try to create a personal relationship with every phone call. The sale was almost secondary.

I have fond memories of Dave, although his recollection of me is probably mixed. One day—I must have been eleven—I accidentally locked the dead bolt on our back door. Up Dave strolled, whistling the theme from *The Bridge on the River Kwai* and—*wham*—he pushed straight into the door and dislocated his shoulder.

# "IRISH AMNESIA" AND MY FIRST ENTREPRENEUR

In another time and another place, my grandmother, Margaret McCann, could have been a major businesswoman. In her own way she was an entrepreneur, a woman entrepreneur, which was very untypical in South Ozone Park. She was strong-willed and never minced words if she had an opinion. She could also talk forever. In those days, when the women regularly outlived their hard-working, hard-drinking husbands, the ladies all had the ability to keep each other company with talk for hours on end.

Most people didn't aspire to have their own businesses. What you wanted was a "safe" job, a place where you could put in your years, retire with a pension, and then maybe work a part-time job for extra money. The best jobs were the union jobs, the skilled trades with a good hourly wage and lots of benefits. The police and the teachers also had good unions with good packages. Next in order of preference were the big institutional jobs at the utilities like the telephone company. Bell Telephone was a very Irish place for a lot of years; to this day, if you look at the upper ranks, you will meet a good number of second- and third-generation Irish.

Grandma had that Irish way of speaking, filtered through New Yorkese. If she said the letter *h* for example, she pronounced it "haitch." The bathroom didn't have a toilet. It had a "terlit." I never met her husband, my grandpa

Frank, who was Irish-born and ran a traditional Irish family. Margaret called Frank "Himself" and he called her "Wife." Grandpa died in his forties, probably of cirrhosis.

Their life revolved around the gin mills and the church. The McCanns did a lot of business with the church and there were always priests around our place.

## MARGARET McCANN'S FIRST LAW OF BUSINESS ETHICS

Grandma McCann was the head of the family and the business. When they were grown, my dad and uncles tried to keep it together for the next generation, but they fought terribly. Some of this was natural sibling rivalry, but a lot of it had to do with money: there wasn't enough. Ours was a marginal business in a not very rich neighborhood. The McCann brothers began to quarrel over scraps, petty quarrels, but those can be as painful and dangerous as wasp stings: a lot of them can kill you. The brothers managed to keep the lid on for some years, but in the end, the resentments mounted up. The business broke up and the bad feelings were devastating. One of my uncles didn't speak with the rest of the family for years. Since my father died, there has been some reconciliation among the surviving brothers. What a shame that it took so long.

"The Irish forget everything except a grudge," my grandmother explained. "Irish amnesia."

It was like in *Godfather II* when Michael Corleone says,

"My brother Alfredo? I have no brother Alfredo. Alfredo is dead." Some uncles and aunts were never mentioned again. They might as well have been dead. It was harsh, and it affected us all terribly.

But if we don't forget a grudge, we also never forget a kindness. This was something Grandma drilled into me until it was second nature, part of her larger business view. These days you may hear it said of a successful businessperson, "He's an animal in business, mean as a snake. But after work or out on the golf course, he's a real gent. Nice as can be, lots of fun."

I can see Margaret McCann right now, pulling herself up to her full five-foot-three and looking down her nose through the line in her bifocals like a hunter sighting in a deer rifle: "Baloney, Jimmy. You are what you are and you don't change who you are just because it's business!"

Apart from it being the right thing to do, my grandmother was of the opinion (and experience has borne this out) that while it is true that money will get you through the good times, this is no test of anything. Anybody can make do when things are flush. Loyalty is the thing that will help you through the bad times.

"Friends" flock to money like flies to cow pies. Now that we are well known for our internet successes and my gray sandy beard and receding hairline run in double-truck ads in *Time* and *Forbes*, you would be amazed how many "really good old friends" I have, all of whom have a "really good deal" for me.

We didn't have too many great deals coming our way

when we started. It was just me, my brother Chris, and (off and on) my sisters and some friends we did business with. We helped each other out. And, as Grandma taught us, you remember *every* time someone is good to you. You remember if someone was good to your father or your grandfather and—here's the good side of Irish amnesia—you *never* forget it.

Grandma brought this home to me years later when my flower business began to take off. I was receiving a lot of pressure and offers of a very good deal to go with a certain wholesaler. It would have meant changing wholesalers and leaving Bernie Lynch, a sweetheart of a guy, who ran a two-man operation on West 28th Street in Manhattan's wholesale flower district.

Businesswise—make that purely for the money—it made sense to move on from Bernie. But, as Grandma pointed out, Bernie had carried me and never demanded a payment when I first started in the flower business, when the money was tight and I couldn't pay my bills. "You repay loyalty with loyalty," she said. And there was no question about it. I stayed with Bernie.

In business, people judge you on a whole array of evidence. They form an opinion about what kind of a person you are. And they can see if you are counterfeit or not. Your suppliers can see it. Your customers can see it. Your employees can see it. You are either known as a stand-up guy or you are not. If you are, you can demand more sacrifice at the shop, expect to be cut some slack from your suppliers when you are caught in a crunch, and know that in any deal your word will count as your bond. People know who they are dealing with and what his or her code is, and they can make rational, bankable business judgments based on a person's character.

You cannot have a more valuable asset.

## Chapter Two

# The New Retail Paradigm

I was in Manhattan recently with a couple of hours between meetings, so I took a walk up Madison Avenue. It was one of those perfect days in New York when all the sidewalk tables at the trendy cafes are filled with trendy people. All the women look like Elle MacPherson as they smile and toss their long hair out of their eyes like supermodels who know they are beautiful and don't have to improve a whole lot on what God gave them. The guys with them are young, in shape, with thick heads of slicked-back hair and tinted lenses; they wear their sport coats thrown casually over their shoulders. None of them looks like me or too many people I know.

The stores in this high fashion strip are the boutiques of the world's most select labels. Armani, Versace, Moschino,

Prada—they are all there. The art-directed employees look like they go home to their yachts after work and party with Elton John and Madonna. Having owned my first flower shop not far from here, I know what the rents are per square foot.

But there is nothing in the stores! A couple of hangers, two or three dresses in the windows, and not much more.

As I look over the merchandise I ask myself, "Say they sold everything in the store today, would that be considered a good day?" I suppose the answer would have to be yes, but there is so little merchandising insight and so much overhead I'd be hard-pressed to find out where the margin is in these businesses.

We have lived through a cultural sea change. Shopping is no longer a chore that we endure in order to stock the fridge with milk and the underwear drawer with socks. It is something we do in the same way that we go to concerts, art shows, and restaurants. Where we shop and what the stores are like reflect our images of ourselves. The thinking is, if we are the kind of people who can shop in Calvin Klein's store on Madison Avenue then we are part of the world of the rich, the famous, the beautiful, and, presumably, the happy. Stores no longer simply have to fulfill our immediate material goals. They have to transform us, uplift us, and, most of all, entertain us.

Entertainment and the world of entertainment breed stars. It's no longer just the movie stars who are famous. Bill Gates, Donna Karan, Nike running shoes, and Tommy Hilfiger clothes are all famous in the same *People*-magazine way. The implied deal is, if you and I buy these various products then we enter an endless party, a problemless world of fame. You or I can be a star, or at least feel like one for a few minutes, when we shop in a glamorous, happening store.

Things have really changed from the days when I shopped in Al's Deli on Lefferts Boulevard in South Ozone Park. Soooooo . . . like Peabody, the super-intelligent dog on *Rocky and Bullwinkle*, used to say to Sherman, his "pet" boy . . .

"Set the way back machine for 1963."

## BUSINESS SHOULD NEVER LOOK *TOO* GOOD!

This is the world I come from. The A train runs along the elevated tracks down Liberty Avenue adding a syncopated *oom-sha-la-la-la-la-click-clack* to the 24-hour-a-day street noise: pickup basketball games, garbage trucks, garbage cans being heaved, babies crying, schoolgirls giggling and playing jump rope, the *pfft* of beer cans being opened by men on their front stoops. Under the "El" a row of small stores makes up the heart of the neighborhood (make that the commercial heart, because the spiritual heart is Our Lady of Perpetual Help). The stores are clean but not overly spiffy. You don't want your shop to look like it is doing *too* well (even if it is) because that would be rubbing your good fortune and prosperity in people's faces. If you put in a new counter or display case, you would have to spend money for them; the money would have to come from somewhere, and the only place you made money was in your store, so you would have to raise your prices and nobody wants to pay more money for eggs so that some hotshot storekeeper can have a new display case.

No, you keep your store clean and your prices down. People come in, make a few purchases, talk about the weather or make fun of the Mets, and leave.

Over here, at 109-57 Lefferts Boulevard, there's Dave and Betty's candy store, my friends' favorite place. Dave and Betty sell newspapers and magazines (they keep the *Playboys* behind the counter). They sell Spaldines, those pink rubber balls that are perfect for playing stickball, and if Tommy Hammil hits a hard line drive and it bounces off the windshield of Glenna Murphy's Buick Roadmaster, nobody's parents have to find the money for a new windshield because the Spaldine is soft and safe. Dave and Betty also sell Imperial Yo-Yos, all fiberglass and shiny. When you are nine years old and have a buck to blow on a good time, those yo-yos fulfill the same kind of product lust that in later years you'll reserve for a new Harley or, later still, a loaded Lexus.

## JIMMY MAC GETS THE BUSINESS BUG

And then there is Al's Deli. Al has a uniform: a white apron and white T-shirt. It could be ninety-five and humid or twelve degrees below zero, but Al has on the same apron and T-shirt. Al has one of those pincer grabbers that he uses to knock the toilet paper off the top shelf and send it tumbling for him to scoop up with a perfect one-handed Willie Mays–style basket catch (in the eternal debate on the relative greatness of Mantle vs. Mays, I am firmly in the Mays camp). Years later I realized why the toilet paper and the Kleenex were always on the top shelf. Did you ever think what it would feel like to catch a number 10 can of tomato juice as it toppled down from a height of ten feet?

Al gives credit. He has this book and if your family is over the limit he tells you, "There's no more room in the book." Translation: "Have your mom come see me when your dad brings home the next paycheck."

Like I said, the other kids all think Dave and Betty's candy store is the cool place in the neighborhood, but I like Al's. My sister Julie says it is from Al that I get my love of business. The thing I love the most is how Al totals up your purchases. No computer, no adding machine. Al has a pencil, a paper bag, and a knife.

You come in and choose your ten or fifteen items. A can of tuna fish . . . a box of Kellogg's Frosted Flakes . . . a roll of toilet paper (never more than one roll at a time) . . . a pack of Pall Malls for Mom (I didn't know then that they would make her so sick). Al lines up the goods and then, like King Richard the Lionhearted dubbing a knight with his broadsword, taps each item with the eraser end of his pencil. Then he takes out his knife and whittles down a new point on his pencil. He writes down the price of every item on a brown paper bag and then counts up the entries, making sure the number of items that he taps equals the number of items on the counter. Then, with a great flourish, he draws a thick black line under the column of figures.

This is Al's magic. Marching down the line of figures with his pencil, he performs the fastest calculation I have ever seen. Even today, it doesn't honestly seem to have been much slower than a computer. Al sure is slick with that pencil. And he's always right. When he's done adding, he snaps open the paper bag with a crisp flourish until it gives a pop that sounds like my Roy Rogers cap pistol.

I do business at 1-800-FLOWERS the way Al did business. Sure, we have enough technology to make old Al's head spin. We have a wide area network based on frame relay technology, a telephone network based on Definity G3RV4 PBX's, TOPMS/ ICP dynamic call routing, and system architecture with Oracle databases, a data warehouse and datamarts, all on a TCP/IP high-speed fiber-optic backbone. I can't tell you precisely what all of it does. I do know, however, that it has cost millions of dollars so far and will cost us more in the future. I am not sure why this is so, but somehow the price tag never shrinks.

Al's technology, on the other hand, was just a step above a charred stick on the wall of a cave. Still, no matter how far technology takes us, it is worth remembering that the basic principles of successful retail were present at Al's Deli.

- Stock the goods that people need.
- Know when to extend credit and how to establish limits.
- Have a way of recording and checking each purchase.
- Did I say "Have a relationship" yet? That should have been first. Remember birthdays, weddings, Little League championships, college scholarships. Make a big deal of them. If you do, you'll never lose your customers. The great food writer and gourmet, James Beard, once said, "A great restaurant is any place where they know your name." People feel that way about any business.

# THE DINOSAUR AND THE
# FIELD MOUSE

I remember a poster that hung on the back wall in Miss Metz's fifth-grade class at Our Lady of Perpetual Help. It was a great gathering of animals from the heyday of the dinosaurs. A couple of volcanoes spouted off in the background. Fern trees as big as oaks soared up from the wet steamy plain. A brontosaurus or two grazed in the swamp, their mouths full of dripping water plants. On the shoreline one of those armored triceratops (they looked like pinheaded rhinos) went mano-a-mano with a T. rex. Scuttling around like seven-year-olds at Thanksgiving dinners was a pack of skinny, razor-toothed little dinosaurs hunting for this and that and trying to stay out of the way of the big guys.

And way, way down in the underbrush there were a couple of ratty-looking critters with mangy fur. These were the First Mammals. All of us fifth-graders knew something that the big meat eaters back then didn't. The dinosaurs were the walking dead. The future belonged to the rats in the bushes.

Back in the early sixties, the retail business and the workplace in general were still ruled by the dinosaurs. Products were simpler. There were fewer choices. Fun—shopping for fun, products that were fun, having fun at work—wasn't part of the general game plan yet. We were a long way from the age of Commerce as Entertainment. But, just like those first mammals in the lower right-hand corner of Miss Metz's poster, the first harbingers of the coming age were already scuttling around under our noses.

When I was in my teens, busting my hump in the family business, there were these two Middle Eastern brothers who ran a clothing store. The store was very hip. A big stereo system blasted the Doors, the Rolling Stones, and the Beatles. There were Nehru jackets and tie-dyed tank tops, bell-bottom jeans, and Beatle boots. Also very expensive mod suits. All of a sudden, shopping was fun. You might even meet girls at Groove City (God help me: that's what they called it).

The storekeepers, Hassan and Ali B'aamscha, were two cool dudes. They wore gold chains emblazoned with their zodiac signs. They drove Bentleys. They had a lifestyle that we all aspired to. They may have had only one customer a day, *but they looked like they were happening*. The only problem was, Hassan and Ali couldn't pay their bills. Within a year they were out of business.

Groove City was about twenty years ahead of its time.


## TAKE MY SNEAKERS . . . PLEASE!

Like those first scrawny mammals, the B'aamscha brothers represented the wave of the future. As we approach the millennium, we want to be entertained when we shop. We want to spend our money not only on goods, but on goods that indicate a certain lifestyle.

For example, when I was growing up in Queens there were two sneaker choices: high-tops or low-tops. They both cost $6.95. P. F. Flyers were first, Keds second, but to us the Keds sticker was not cool, worse than a scarlet A. But today, as I write these words, I wouldn't dream of buying a pair of plain old sneakers. First, my kids would have nothing to do with me, and, second, there are no such things as plain old sneakers anymore. Am I looking for running shoes, walking shoes, cross-trainers, basketball shoes, paddleball shoes? Do I want them high or low, with air or without? Do they need fluorescent strips on the heels so my neighbors can see me jogging at night and not sideswipe me as they zip by in their BMWs? And, most of all, would I be insane enough to entrust the only pair of feet I will ever have to a pair of shoes that cost less than $100?

Once upon a time the answer would have been "Are you kidding? You can buy new feet for $100!" But now athletic shoes are part of a lifestyle. If I can't be like Mike, at least my shoes can look like his. Going shopping for shoes has become a whole new fun activity—it's entertainment. Unquestionably, the home runs in retail in the past ten years have, in one way or another, incorporated entertainment. The Gap pipes in good music and has friendly, terrific-looking young people to help you. The Disney and the Warner stores, the Virgin store in Times Square, Nike Town: you don't simply go there to buy there. You also go there to *be there*.

At 1-800-FLOWERS I believe that one of the keys to our success in the world of telemarketing has been creating a place where people want to be electronically. When we first bought the business, it really was a lousy deal: several million dollars of debt and a telephone number, and not a telephone number with a very good track record if you stop to think about it. After all, you don't go millions in the red if everything is going great. We had to overcome all kinds of resistance to get people to do something as personal as buying flowers over the telephone for someone they really care about.

We had to do a lot of things right, and we needed a lot of luck. But friendliness and genuine interest in the customer were certainly among the most important elements in our growth. A lot of that had to do with hiring people who like people, people who can send a smile over the telephone.

Later, when we got into on-line commerce, we had to give people a reason to want to be in our virtual store. Even though the internet is growing, the fact remains that, as with 800 numbers, people didn't start out flocking to the internet as a retail outlet. In fact, in the face of a tsunami of hype, they basically yawned and took their dollars to more traditional outlets. 1-800-FLOWERS, however, was the fastest-growing company on the internet. I think the main reason is we learned our lesson ten years earlier in telemarketing. We had to add something to the value equation to make people want to come to our site, and that something was personal contact and entertainment.

And now the circle goes round. Three years ago we bought the big West Coast flower chain, Conroy's. From virtual stores we are now back to a four-physical-walls flower business with real physical people.

Nike is no longer just a shoe. 1-800-FLOWERS is no longer just a telephone number. They are both brands. The new retail paradigm sends the shoppers to destinations where they can buy the goods, and the purchase is validated by the reputation of your brand.

## ARE WE HAVING
## ANY FUN YET?

I went to a Catholic high school in Bedford Stuyvesant, one of Brooklyn's famously tough neighborhoods. Somehow I ended up in a typing class with some of the wilder kids. Brother Lewis, at age eighty-two, was in charge of this rambunctious bunch of city kids. He teetered down the aisles in his ancient cassock. As kids will, we referred to him as "a walking holiday." Cruel as it sounds, we figured, "Eighty-two years old, ill health—this guy is going to check out any day, and we'll be off from school for the funeral."

Guess what? Brother Lewis, all five-foot-five and I'm guessing 150 pounds, may have been assigned the worst-behaved kids in school (I swear it was all a mistake in my case), but he also had the class with the best attendance record.

His secret? Fun. When people have fun, they work better, get along better, come back for more. Brother Lewis's unlikely fun weapon was one of those blue stickers that used to come on bunches of Chiquita Bananas. Brother Lewis would prowl the typing class with a roll of those stickers and whenever he saw you doing something right, he would place a sticker on your forehead. Now, this might pass for playful silliness in the suburbs. But in our Bed Stuy school, when you met Nick DeTroleo, who carried a zip gun under his sweater and a knife tied around his ankle, your first instinct wasn't to think, "Here's a guy who wants a blue Chiquita Banana sticker on his head." I am sure that when Nick was in grade school, he was the kid who would pull the wings off of flies. I still remember marveling one day when Nick earned a row of blue stickers on his forehead and marched out of Brother Lewis's schoolroom beaming with pride.

Brother Lewis's secret to Nick-taming was that he had found a way to make a mundane, boring class more interesting. He made a connection. Though it may sound silly and just a tad unsophisticated to you, we are all, deep down, pretty silly and unsophisticated creatures. Little fun things can be all the difference between a blah job and a place you don't mind spending time in.

Years later, my brother Chris hired Vinnie McVeigh, who was an Irish city kid like us. He, like his whole family, was on the police force. Being a cop is one of those occupations that fits the New York Irish genetic profile. One day in Bed Stuy, Vinnie was chasing down what in cop lingo is known as a perp. When he caught up with him in a deserted alley, he tackled the guy, who apparently didn't want to be tackled because he began to whale on Vinnie with great gusto. Finally, Vinnie cuffed the guy. He paused and looked down at his uniform, which was all ripped and bloody. Right then and there he had one of those life-clarifying moments.

"Do I really want to be doing this for another fifteen years?" Vinnie asked himself. Even though his father and some of his brothers and uncles were lifers on the force (and great cops), Vinnie realized he didn't have to stay on forever.

So he quit the force, went to work selling Hyundais and somehow ended up with us. Actually, I shouldn't toss off the word "somehow," like it was an accident. Vinnie, Chris, and I came from the same type of neighborhood, with the same values, and he was the kind of guy we instantly connected with. One day, when we were sharing Bedford Stuyvesant experiences, I told him about Brother Lewis and the Chiquita Banana stickers.

When Vinnie came to 1-800-FLOWERS, we put him to work in our telecenter, where he could make some money exercising his Gaelic gift for gab. It also crossed my mind that having a street-toughened New York cop, straight out of the ghetto, wouldn't hurt the decorum and good order of the place. So no one was more surprised than I when I popped into the Worcester telecenter one day and saw Vinnie walking up and down the rows of telereps, pausing now and again, without saying a word, to put one of those have-a-nice-day smiley face stickers on a telerep's computer terminal.

"Stra-a-a-nge puppy," I said to myself. Even though I was the one who told him about Brother Lewis, I was as mystified as our telereps. At least back in school with Brother Lewis, we knew what he was doing, but Vinnie didn't explain a thing. He just kept at it till some reps had a dozen stickers, while some had none.

Slowly, it began to dawn on people what Vinnie was up to. He was looking for smiles. When he saw somebody smiling while talking on the telephone, he put a sticker on their terminal. By the end of that shift, we had a regular love fest going on at the telecenter, and I knew we had a real prize in Vincent McVeigh. He had come up with a cute, innovative way to say, "This is the behavior I want to see. It will make your day more fun and it will make our customers' experience more fun." Fun at work makes work more pleasant, makes us more successful in establishing a bond with our customers. Believe it or not, I really feel that a customer can almost feel you smiling over the phone line. The sticker was the reward for fun, and, ever since I earned my first quarter helping my grandma, I have never gone into a business that didn't have an element of fun.

## YOUR OFFICE NEEDS MY GRANDMOTHER'S KITCHEN

Painting houses and churches is wearying work. In my dad's words, "We had to bust our shoes." We looked for ways to lighten up the day. Otherwise it would have been eight or more hours of dirt and paint and turpentine and cleaning brushes and sweat and more dirt. If I have fond memories of those days, it is not of the work itself. In fact, my distaste for it was one of the reasons that I tried a number of other jobs and, in the end, discovered I wasn't really looking for work: I was looking for my own business. My quest was an act of survival. As an entrepreneur I have continued to learn lessons about the basics of survival. In the beginning, we were always on such thin ice as a business, every decision was a critical one. This probably explains why I have never spent a lot of money on a fancy office or battalions of assistants for our executives (we have four secretaries in our company of 2,000 employees).

But I have never stinted on having a little fun like we had in the old days in Queens. The things I remember most fondly about my grandmother's (and then my father's) business are the times we would get together to shoot the breeze, hang out, plan the next day's work. In the mornings, first thing, we would all meet at Grandma's. That was the home office, just a semi-attached brick and frame house with a long driveway. We had a row of garages for storage.

The men would gather at 6:15 and have coffee and donuts around Grandma's table. I especially remember Hank, who was the size of a Steinway piano and an amazing painter, twice as fast and better than the rest of us. Hank's only problem was he had a lot of problems. If he wasn't in trouble with the law, then it was some gang or other that was after him. But on the job, he was rock solid.

And then there was Rip, who may have had a normal first and last name, but I never knew it. He was a sweetheart and big as they come. He was broad across the chest, and his big head and thick neck looked like they were bolted onto his body. Rip's particular specialty (make that handicap) was giving directions. He reminded me of the guy on the old Federal Express commercials who used to talk a mile a minute. Rip was that way with directions. He gave the most detailed directions, with one critical drawback: he had a mental block when it came to street names—he couldn't remember them.

"Hey, Rip, how do I get to Holy Name?"

Rip would look up, think a second, and then he would click in: "Two stoplights past Herzog's bakery, a left goes down this hill, it curves twice and then there is that green house where they keep the Christmas lights on all year. Keep going straight, over the big street."

"Which big street, Rip? Queens Boulevard?" (As its name suggests, it's the biggest street in Queens.)

"I dunno, yeah, maybe. So anyway you come to the bodega with the *Vote for Mario Biaggi* sticker in the window" . . . and on . . . and on. You had to be careful when you asked Rip how to get someplace. It could be an all-morning proposition.

Rip and Hank and my dad and my uncles (in the years when they were on speaking terms) were a close-knit group. My job, when I first started going out with them, was to buy sandwiches, coffee, and sodas for their main meal and breaks. And then, at the end of the day, it was back to Grandma's kitchen.

Everyone would have a Scotch and get mellow, and the conversation flowed. I was just a happy fly on the wall listening to all this grown-up talk. It was a time for camaraderie, for new ideas, for discussion of strategy, for planning new business.

We were a group of people with a shared experience, letting off steam together. There was no plan, no goal for these gatherings, but good ideas came from them, and, just as important, it was bonding time. It certainly was the payoff for me. I remember wondering if I would ever have stories as funny as those kitchen table stories. Their tales of brave exploits in barroom arguments or run-ins with street punks got my heart pounding. I think I have learned, in the years since, that if you are a storytelling type, the same kinds of things will happen to you, and you will enjoy retelling your exploits and screw-ups with the same relish as those Ozone Park painters. I can't help but add that it also helps if you are Irish.

When it came time to plan our 1-800-FLOWERS offices at the current headquarters on Long Island, I was very impressed with the ergonomic design, the layout of the workstations, the expandable computer network. It was terrific, but it lacked one thing: my grandmother's kitchen.

"I want Grandma's kitchen here."

Everybody looked up at me when I said this. I was the boss, so I got their attention and a lot of head scratching and puzzled looks to boot.

So now we have the Margaret McCann Lounge—at least that's what I will always call it. It's a comfy break room with couches and a couple of tables to hang out at and have coffee, pizza, whatever. It is also a great place for me to stop in and shoot the breeze, especially now that I am busier, the company is bigger, and I don't have the easy contact with everyone that I had when we were smaller. If anything, it is more important now than it ever was that I know how the folks on the front line feel and that I get their immediate feedback on what is happening out there at the interface between our customers and our business.

People open up more quickly and are more at ease than they would be if I called them down to my office. The boss's office always feels like the principal's office in school: even if you are called there because the principal has some good news, you always think, "Oh brother, what did I do now?"

But in the break room, we're on common ground, and there is a chance for better dialogue and the opportunity to learn something valuable. The ideas that have come out of the break room have paid for ten thousand break rooms, and somehow they seem to come when the work is most intense and you are at your tiredest, like holiday time, when you are in the seventeenth hour of the workday from hell. It is 1:30 in the morning. The phone traffic is lighter. You take a break. Someone goes to White Castle for a mega-order of belly bombers, and when he returns we all start to download.

Someone says, "You know, what if we reconfigure the credit card cues? We can change the order entry screen to set the data up front before we take the order. Then the credit card hassle is taken care of."

And someone else says, "Yeah, but I would do it differently." And all of a sudden we are grabbing scrap paper from the wastebasket and drawing flowcharts and designs for flower baskets and out of that so-tired-you-couldn't-be-tireder time, we come up with an idea that works. When one of those moments happens, you can see that "there-at-the-creation" glow in everyone's eyes.

One of our biggest-selling items, the Junk Food Gift Basket, happened this way. It was six o'clock in the morning around Christmastime. A big seller then was a Fruit and Gourmet Gift Basket and we had moved a lot of them that day. We were sitting around the break room and one of the gang—speaking straight from the heart, or perhaps the stomach—said, "Oranges and cheese are nice enough, but you know what I would like to get right about now?"

"Two Knicks tickets," a Knicks fan answered.

"A two-thousand-dollar bonus," said a mom whose son had just started college.

"A day off!" someone else said.

"Nope. I would like some Cracker Jacks or potato chips."

Picking up on the idea, my brother chimed in, "I could sure go for a Snickers."

Pretty soon we started to sound like my kids when they used to take inventory of their Halloween haul. What we had here was a serious case of the junk food munchies. I grabbed my keys and went down to the all-night deli and stocked up on Snickers, M&Ms, Reese's Peanut Butter Cups, Charleston Chews . . . I must have looked like I was priming the pump for the American Society for the Propagation of Cavities.

I went over to our nearest retail shop, got out a basket and colored cellophane, and made a beautiful junk food array. Just about then—it must have been nine-thirty in the morning—a customer walked in, took one look at our basket, and said, "That's it. That's just what I want. I'll take it."

Our public had spoken. I felt that specialized retailer's tingle that I get in the presence of a money-making idea. I gave the guy a price, made up another basket for the break room bunch, and the Junk Food Gift Basket was born. It became one of our biggest items until, seventeen years later, another late bull session in a Denver steak house gave birth to the Birthday Flower Cake.

You may not have a grandma's kitchen in your place, but I guarantee that if you build one, the good ideas will come.

## THE FUN MARGIN

I believe with every bit of my soul that fun has value. It is the social glue that can transform a workplace. Face it: work can be—in fact, often is—a drag. It doesn't have to be. I'm not saying that if one of our employees won the lottery, he or she would still come to work every day (although I am proud to say that when Gladys Vasquez won ten million dollars in the lottery, she stayed on with us through the Mother's Day holiday because, as she put it, "These are my friends. This is my world. What else am I going to do?").

As an employer or a manager, you have to put yourself in the shoes of the people who work for you. You have to think about their lives out of the shop. Many of our folks are like Diane from Lake Ronkonkoma. Before she comes to work on the early night shift, she has already picked the kids up from school, cooked dinner, monitored the homework and the toothbrushing, settled a few arguments, and driven to work on the Long Island Expressway (which, I am convinced, is a secret government testing station to find out how much traffic one person can handle before turning into a homicidal psychopath).

When she walks through our doors, the first thing I want her to do is smile. It doesn't matter exactly what it is that we are doing—a barbecue, musicians, or caricature artists—the point is we're trying *something* that people are going to enjoy. Something to lighten the load. When you come into 1-800-FLOWERS, I want you to forget that tough bus ride to work, the broken fan belt on the Toyota, the spouse who was late getting home to take over kid duty. I want to release all of those tensions for a while because if you are relaxed you are going to do your job better. You will interact with your co-workers better. You will definitely do better with customers.

# PROFITS OF DOOM!

If entertainment is taking over our culture, and I believe that it is, then the workplace has to have entertainment value. So much of what we do at work is aimed at stressing the seriousness of it all, the gravity of work. But with very few exceptions it is not as serious as we make it out to be, not as earth-shattering as we claim. I remember visiting a friend who is a top scientist at Bell Labs. He is one of the major players in computerized speech synthesis, which is one intellectually demanding job. However, if you go out to Bell Labs (they call it AT&T Labs now) and it gets to be mid-afternoon, you will not see a lot of speech synthesizing going on. Instead you will see my friend Pieter (I have changed the name to protect the guilty) sitting in front of his computer with a crazed grin on his face. From time to time he grimaces, squints, snorts, and even lets out a curse or two. The computer goes *Zap! Pow! Kaboom!* Pieter and the other future Nobel Prizers on that floor are playing a networked game of Doom.

Think about it: AT&T is paying its speech synthesis scientists zipcodes of dollars per hour. Should they really be playing Doom? Sure they should! It's fun. It relaxes them. It connects them to each other. So even if it looks like kid stuff (and I know that a lot of the things we try at 1-800-FLOWERS are pretty kidlike), you would be surprised at how so-called sophisticated people respond to even the simplest effort at lightening up the situation.

Time to lighten up!

## Chapter Three

# Work = Life

It takes a lot of effort to separate work from the rest of your life. I stopped trying. Actually, I never really started. Because ours was a family business and because the headquarters was my grandmother's house, it wasn't a case of dad going to the office and then coming home and not talking about work. We lived our work.

There was no set time for work or, to put it more accurately, there was no set time for being off from work. Dad was the boss. He kept the big picture in mind. He got the jobs and worked with the suppliers and the other contractors. His brothers were the foremen. They supervised and did the on-site work.

On Sundays, we frequently went over to Grandma's for dinner. Dad would get there two hours early and work up the estimates, dictating them to Grandma. Next morning at seven A.M. the estimates would be all ready. Having had that kind of upbringing, when I am asked, "What is your workday?" all I can say is, "I don't know. It's when I work. Could be anytime. Could be all the time."

I think the ability to be on call, though not necessarily on duty, all the time is a tremendous advantage. If you are an entrepreneur and you do not eat, live, and breathe your business, you will very soon be an ex-entrepreneur. This ability to treat work as part of your life, as opposed to something that you wall off from life, is one of the reasons people have so much trouble competing with us. It is not that we are so much smarter or so much better than anyone else. We are not. Sure, we are good at execution, but so are a lot of people. The real secret is that we *live* this business. Ten or twenty years down the line, we will still be in it. When you have that attitude, no one will outdo you. Someone may come along who will do the job as well as you can, but they are not going to do it better. It's like Woody Allen once said when asked what the secret was to making good movies—something like "Eighty percent of it is showing up." If you show up all the time, you're going to do fine.

Please understand: I am not recommending that you be a workaholic. If you work all the time and spend no time with your family, you will mess up. You will always be tense, on edge, guilty about not being with the kids or, if you are with the kids, being angst-ridden about work. Workaholics are people who are basically insecure: they secretly feel that they are not really up to snuff. They believe that unless they are running around plugging up imaginary holes in the dike, the whole dam will burst and drown them in their own fundamental worthlessness. This, of course, is a lot of baloney. There is no such thing as heading off every crisis. If you worry all the time, you will inevitably screw up. No one can stand that much tension and still maintain efficiency.

The trick is creating a more seamless balance between work and life and not diving into one at the expense of the other. Or, to rework a current phrase, you don't have to get a life if you already have one.

The ability to integrate life with work varies from person to person. A lot depends on your family, especially your spouse. If he or she is supportive, you will be fine. If there is, on the other hand, a constant back and forth pull on your energies, both work and family will suffer. Ours is the kind of business that doesn't let you choose. After all, our busiest times, the days we work the hardest, are the days that other families are spending together having a family meal, watching the football game, going on vacation. Thanksgiving, Christmas, Easter, Mother's Day, you will be sure to find us putting in eighteen-hour days. It's a given. It would not be doable if our wives and husbands didn't accept that this is the way things are.

When we do get together as a family—like very late on Christmas Day or the day *after* Mother's Day—someone will always make a plea that we refrain from talking shop. But I am in the business, my brother Chris is in the business, my sister Julie is in the business, my other siblings, Peggy and Kevin, are often in the business, as well. We all try not to talk shop—for about ten minutes. Then invariably someone will have a comment about Julie's latest TV spot or a story about one of our delivery people going through hell and high water to get a bouquet to a widowed invalid on top of a mountain and, just like that, we are talking shop again.

Work, in the extended McCann family, is not something that the men go off and do by themselves. For starters, my two sisters are very much in the picture and they are decidedly not men. But beyond that, as entrepreneurs, we don't see business as something we should try to keep out of the home because it's not pleasant and fun to talk about. We love our work. And once you can get beyond trying to maintain arbitrary boundaries between work and the rest of your life, it gets a lot more bearable when you have to work those long hours. It becomes more of a communal experience that you embrace and enjoy rather than one that, in the old-fashioned way of doing things, you try to hide from the wife and kids.

## THE ANDREWS SISTERS, BUDDY HACKETT, AND MY DAD

My dad was a networker before people thought of using the word. Early on, he realized that the contracting business—like every business I have ever known—is a relationship business. If the monsignor at St. Agnes likes your jokes, and if you listen when he tells you to lighten the color in the rectory kitchen, then he is going to tell Father Meara at Trinity whose brother, John, owns two apartment buildings in Bay Ridge, and so it goes.

Dad was particularly good at glad-handing. My sister Julie says that's where I get it from. Every year in the hottest days of summer (when it's too hot to perch on a scaffold and paint) the Painting and Decorating Contractors of America would have a convention up in some Catskill resort where Buddy Hackett or Imogene Coca or the Andrews Sisters were the headliners. It seems it was always one of those Borscht Belt places in what used to be called the Jewish Alps, where even a bunch of Irish and Italian contractors could count on cold borscht, hot blintzes, and potato knishes.

For my dad, who eventually became president of the Painting and Decorating Contractors of America, these conventions were a refuge from the day-to-day grind. When things started to go sour with his brothers, the conventions became a place to pursue the business away from the constant tension, a chance to play on a different stage. For me it was a chance to get out and see something different from our little corner of the world.

I am reminded of those upstate treks whenever I accept an invitation to give my spiel for different business groups. I get something out of them in the same way my dad did at those conventions: new friends, new customers, new opportunities, new ideas. And I get something else out of these trips, something I'm sure my dad did too. But he was so good at keeping things inside and never letting us kids know that he had emotions that it wasn't until I had children of my own and began to take them on the road that I could look back and, in my memory, see my dad's face again and read the emotions that he hid so well.

## TAKE THE KIDS

A recent trip that I took with my son, Jimmy, stirred memories of a trip I took with my dad to Binghampton, at that time a down-at-the-heels upstate New York industrial town. There was this fellow, Bob Gray, who was a CPA and professor of accounting at the state university up there. He was also an airplane pilot. My dad had no special agenda in taking me beyond wanting me to meet someone who could be a role model.

Well, I had the same thought when I joined the board of Gateway Computers. Ted Waitt, the founder, has a ponytail, drives a Porsche, and listens to loud rock music. I wanted Jimmy to see that there were all kinds of guys and gals in the business world. It wasn't all shirt-and-tie types.

Jimmy really liked Ted and vice versa. But the guy who made the real impression on my son was Jim Taylor, the head of marketing at Gateway.

Years earlier, Taylor had been one of those students at Berkeley who was making a lifetime career out of school. There he was, rolling along, avoiding real life, when the school suggested to him that he had accidentally matriculated, so why didn't he just graduate and get started with life? He did, becoming one of the true marketing gurus in the nation (and I believe that some of Gateway's recent success tells you something about his talents).

My son and Jim Taylor hit it off right away. Maybe it was Jim's absentminded-professor manner. And when I say "absentminded" I really do mean major league forgetful. That day, Taylor took us to lunch, paid the check, and got into his car before he noticed that he had forgotten his shoes in the restaurant! (Jim is famous for sliding his shoes off whenever and wherever he sits down.) Come to think of it, he didn't notice. It was Jimmy who cleared his throat and asked, "Uh, Dr. Taylor, did you mean to leave your shoes as a tip?"

Next, on the way to the airport, my son noticed a flashing light on the dashboard and said, "Uh, Dr. Taylor, I think you are out of gas." Smart as he is, sometimes I think Jim Taylor is the Christopher Lloyd of the real world.

It was a treat for me to travel with my son, to expose him to new things, and to show him that there is a whole country out there between the two coasts—in fact, most of America. The next year I was helping Jimmy pack up for school and I noticed he had my copy of Jim Taylor's book, *The 500 Year Delta*, which is an extremely deep book about how the world has changed and will continue to change in the coming centuries. I knew that Jimmy had enjoyed our trip to Gateway because he didn't complain once that day. But when I saw him actually starting to study, on his own time, the stuff that I thought was important, I also realized that there are benefits on several levels to the quality one-on-one time together this type of trip with the kids affords. I know it worked for me with my dad.

My dad would have loved it if we could have had the day

that my son Matt and I had a couple of springs ago. I had been involved with literacy programs for some time. I can't overemphasize how fundamentally important I find it. Literacy is the key to acquiring a marketable skill, especially in the cyber age. Without it you are in danger of becoming an "information have-not" while the rest of society is full of "information haves."

As part of my community work, I've worked with a terrific literacy program called Reading Is Fundamental. I had to go down to Orlando to shoot a public service announcement with Shaquille O'Neal (this was before he became a Laker), who also is a big-time pro-literacy advocate. We had to film on a Monday because that was Shaq's only day off. As I was waiting for the cab to come and pick me up for my ride to the airport, I talked to my son Matt before he ran out the door to play some hoops with his friends. Matt, by the way, is a major b-ball fan.

"How are you doing in school?" I asked. "Are you behind in anything?"

"Actually I am all caught up and things seem to be going pretty good this year, Dad," he answered, telling me what I already knew.

"Have you missed any days?" I continued.

"I think maybe two, when I had that stomach thing. Why do you ask?"

"Matt, you know where I am going today?"

"Yeah, to do a commercial with Shaq."

"Well, since you are doing so well in school and haven't missed very much, would you like to join me?"

Moving as fast as I have ever seen him move, Matt was

out of the room and back with his gym bag at twice the speed of light.

Shaquille O'Neal, who is a very friendly person, took the time to kid around with Matt, and I even got a picture of the two of them with Shaq holding my son against his hip just like he was a sack of potatoes. Matt was in heaven. He walked around with such a big ear-to-ear grin all day that I was worried he was going to sprain his cheeks.

The real payoff for me came on the plane, in our hotel room, during dinner at Planet Hollywood, and going back and forth to the airport. We got a chance to talk, just the two of us. Nothing earthshaking, but a great opportunity to spend some time away from the rest of our daily world.

I remember Matt turning to me on the plane ride home and asking, "Dad, do you love what you do?"

"What do you mean?"

"Do you love your work?"

"I do, Matt."

"Well, you know, Dad, when I hear my friends' fathers, they sometimes talk about how they can't wait until the weekend, and you never talk like that. I can never tell when you're on vacation because it's usually involved with business and the whole family goes. It all seems to be part of the same thing."

Work = life. Life = work. Matt was right: they are all part of the same thing. I share this story with you not because I expect all of you to own a company like ours, although I am sure that some of you will. Nor do I expect that most of you will get to take your kid to spend a day with his sports idol. My real point is that the ability to integrate work and the rest of your life allows you to be more productive in both areas. Or, to put it in more businesslike terms, you have a finite amount of emotional capital to invest. If you divide it up between your professional and personal life, you will have two small investments. If you succeed in blending the two, you can pool your resources of capital to gain some very productive economies of scale.

## Chapter Four

# Sharp-Dressed Man

## IN PRAISE OF PRAISE

It was the summer of my freshman year in high school. I was working for my dad, as I had done every summer since grammar school. We were on a job out in Flatlands in Brooklyn on one of those hot summer days when the sun bakes the sidewalk and concrete, the air gets steamy, and the only difference between shade and sun is that the shade is dark and hot and the sun is light and hot. In the natural order of things, man was not created to stand on a scaffold having his brains bake as he inhales paint fumes.

It was a big job, a parochial school, so we had taken on extra help. I think there were at least twenty-five guys on our crew. Being the boss's son, according to my father, qualified me to do all of the crummiest chores. Maybe that's why I so fondly remember our breaks and driving to work in the truck and hearing the guys hooting and hollering, usually over some pretty girl as she crossed the street.

Once we got to the site, I would work on taping the woodwork, dropping the light fixtures from the ceilings. Then I would lay the drop cloths, do some spackling and sanding (which no one else ever wanted to do). Then, as an extra special penance for every sin I had ever committed— and got away with—I was also called upon to wash the brushes.

One morning, about ten A.M., I was walking down this Brooklyn street going for coffee. I was already pretty grimed up, with lots of plaster and paint drippings on my work clothes. It was a two-block walk—just long enough to start to feel really clammy. I kept humming a Lovin' Spoonful song:

*Hot time, summer in the city*

I was feeling pretty fed up with life when I walked by a haberdashery (there's a word you don't see anymore). There was this very sharp dude wearing an extremely cool shirt and tie and crisply pressed slacks. He was whisk-brooming a few microspecks of dust from his lapel as he got ready to open the store.

"Jeez," I thought to myself. "Here it is, ten o'clock in the morning, and I've been busting my shoes for four hours [in the summer we left home super early to try and get a good amount of work in before the heat of the day] and this guy is cool, calm, and collected, not a drop of sweat on him, just getting ready to open his shop!"

It was at that precise moment that I knew I had to change my life. I wanted to be like that guy. In fact, I wanted to be that guy. Seen from all possible angles, working in a clothing store seemed to be the perfect job. Up to that time, clothes had never been that important to me. They were just functional. Every year I would get two pairs of jeans at the beginning of the school year. If they wore out in the knees or crotch from playing basketball with my buddies, I would have to make do with iron-on patches or a few quick stitches. But, with the coming of the Beatles and bell-bottoms, clothes became cool and interesting. And if you wanted any girl to take an interest in you, there was no percentage in tooling around looking like a loser. You needed some cool threads.

If I worked in a clothing store, I reasoned, not only would I not have to lug scaffolds and paintbrushes around the five boroughs, I would also get a discount on clothes. The only job that could possibly rival that would be tending bar and getting to drink draft beer for free.

It just so happened that our neighborhood had a clothing store, Dadson's, on Liberty Avenue. It was owned by Ebb Weissman. Ebb was the son of Russian immigrants who had owned a "corseteria." What a word! I've never seen a corseteria outside of New York, but when I was a kid, every neighborhood had one. They sold bras, girdles, and a general line of what were called "foundation garments." When I first heard this term, the only meaning I knew for the word "foundation" was something massive and made out of cement. It would have taken nothing less to slim down some of the ladies on our block. When girls started burning their bras as a sign of women's lib, I am sure many of our local matrons were horrified, but also perhaps a little pleased as society lightened up on its requirements in the area of clothes as instruments of torture.

So Ebb went into the family business while his brother Joe became a well-known character actor in movies. In one of the high points of the history of our neighborhood, brother Joe played Dr. No in the James Bond movie of the same name. By the time Ebb hired me, he had a very prosperous little business. Actually, for our neighborhood, it wasn't that little. He started with one small shop. Then he bought the building next door, and the one next to that, and I think he was probably up to four buildings when I went to work for him.

I learned a lot about business from Ebb. I also learned a lot in spite of him.

## PRAISE? YOU MUST BE KIDDING!

Ebb's management style was very simple: "You show up and do the work and I pay you." My dad held similar views. They used to say that men should never show emotions, certainly never a soft or caring one. These guys subscribed to that notion, chapter and verse. Ebb worked hard. He wanted you to work hard. In all the time I spent with him, on and off for ten years, I can honestly say that I cannot recall one word of praise. Not getting yelled at was praise enough. Or maybe you got a twenty-five-cent-an-hour raise. God forbid, however, that you should ask for that raise. "You want a raise?" he would say. "I'll give you a raise down!"

It was the same thing working for my dad. Jim McCann Sr. was a big guy: six feet and handsome. When he was young, he was a lineman in semipro football. Praise was not in his vocabulary. I remember my dad asking me to clean up the shop, which was in a bunch of garages in back of Grandma's. I started cleaning brushes, taking apart pumps and cleaning and oiling the parts, putting the drop cloths away, separating the tools, hanging them on their own hooks. I felt like Mickey Mouse in *The Sorcerer's Apprentice*.

When I was finished, ten hours later, I called my dad in and he looked over the whole job. He went from spot to spot and never really said anything. That was good: if he spoke it would have been to point out a mistake. At the end, he gave the shop a once-over and said something like, "How come you hung the roller handles over there? Now I'll have to reach across the bench to get to them."

That was as close as Dad (or Ebb) ever got to praise.

## THE PRINCE OF TIDES (IN LONGHAND)

In a family or in business, I am very conscious of the emotional message that a word from the boss carries. Whether it's praise, encouragement, idle chitchat, or, more rarely, censure, it is important to remember, and never forget, that a manager's words carry extra weight. I have seen this time and again in business: an offhand comment stays with somebody for months, even years, because it came from The Boss. This is true no matter what business you are in, as I learned on a trip to Ireland. President Clinton was going over for his first trip there to try and further the peace process and had invited a whole planeload of Irish-American notables.

On that trip I hung out a lot with Pat Conroy, who wrote *The Prince of Tides* and *The Great Santini*, among other books. I had always liked his stuff and I liked him even more—a bubbly, fun guy with a touch of the mischievous elf in him. He had seen me appear in some Apple computer ads, and, as we chatted, the subject of computers came up. Was I ever surprised when it turned out that this major author wrote completely in longhand.

No computer. Not even a typewriter.

This is something that I find truly alarming and fear-inspiring. How can you write something without crossing out and changing it a million times?

"Since you read *The Great Santini*," he explained, "you know it was about my dad."

For those of you who haven't read the book, Pat Conroy's dad, a Marine colonel, was the all-time strict dad.

"When I was in high school in the Carolinas, my dad called me into his office one day. 'Pat,' he said, 'are you a homosexual?'

" ' I don't think so,' I managed to get out."

Pat added that this was well before our more enlightened time of don't ask, don't tell (or, who cares anyway?), which wouldn't have made a whole lot of difference anyway to Pat's very unenlightened dad.

"I have come to understand that you registered in a typing class," the Great Santini said. "Well, no son of mine takes typing. That's for homosexuals."

Pat's father called the principal and had Pat taken out of the class, and Pat developed a phobia about typing from which he never recovered. Moral of the story: when you are in the position of a superior—Commanding Officer, Parent, or Employer—your words can have a tremendous effect in developing attitudes and skills.

# I READ IT ON THE REFRIGERATOR DOOR

Ebb, my dad, the Great Santini—men of that era didn't cry, and they didn't praise somebody face-to-face. Too much emotion. Sign of weakness. Other guys will take advantage of you.

I am glad I had that lesson drummed into me so well, because it is one that I try to break at least once a day. The simple fact of the matter is, praise is one of the most effective management tools there is. Think about it. When our kids take their first baby steps, do we tell them offhandedly, "Oh, that's nice. Look, I'm a little busy now, can you save that for another time?"

No, you praise your child. You hug, and kiss, and clap, and keep on doing it. Encouragement and praise go a long way with kids. Grown-ups too.

At 1-800-FLOWERS we have gone back to one of the most effective forms of public praise that I recall from childhood. It came about when we were discussing the need to monitor calls to make sure that our service and friendliness messages were getting across effectively. Monitoring is one of those words that can make any employee nervous. "Why are they monitoring me? What did I do wrong?"

Actually it had very little to do with anybody doing anything wrong. We pretty much know, before we put them to work, that our telereps have a phone-friendly manner. Monitoring reveals strengths to share with others as well as giving us clues on how to sharpen our message and improve our service.

Faye Pannell, who had been one of our friendliest and most effective telereps, was at that time running our telemarketing operation from her command post in the telecenter.

"What did your mother do when you came home with a good report from school?" Faye asked, then answered her own question: "She put in on the refrigerator door with one of those little magnets."

Now you may think that magnets on the refrigerator door is a bit corny for grown-ups. You're right, but that's the way I like things. When you make a corny gesture, people get it. It makes them smile and drives the message home. The very next Saturday, Chris and I went to Joe's Junk Yard behind Liberty Avenue in Jamaica, and we bought a

Frigidaire door. We mounted it on the wall at the entrance to the telecenter. Whenever we found somebody doing something noteworthy during a monitored call, Faye would write it up and stick her letter of commendation on the refrigerator door, giving due recognition for a job well done.

People really liked that door. They used to look at it as soon as they came on duty. You could see them checking to see if they were there. And more than a few times, when people thought they were unobserved, I would see them casually rearrange the notices on the door so that theirs was on top.

It got people talking, responding. Sure, it was a little Mickey Mouse, and there came a time when it had done all the good it was going to do, but that refrigerator door was another way to make contact and, in so doing, to make people feel good about the job and themselves.

## THE CASH REGISTER
## LOTTERY

Sometimes, to pass the time at Dadson's we had a pool to see who could turn the toughest customer, or who could sell the worst-looking item in the shop. Say we had a horrendous paisley Nehru jacket that hadn't sold for three months: we'd have a wager one day where each of us would take a shot at selling it. We had one regular customer who worked for the parks department—a real sweetheart but not exactly a brain surgeon. He was of the opinion that the problem of his nonexistent love life would be solved by the right choice of clothes. He would take anything if you promised him it would attract women. Whenever he came in, you knew that whoever was on deck was going to try to sell him one of the loser items.

We also competed for high sales for the day. This required some sophisticated information gathering. When I say that Ebb Weissman didn't give praise freely, or at all, I don't mean to give the impression that he was talkative about everything else. When it came to the state of his business, it was none of our business. If you asked him, it didn't matter that merchandise had been flying out the doors. Ebb would always glance heavenward, give a depressed shrug of the shoulders, and let go a world-weary sigh that was meant to signify that we were holding on by the skin of our teeth and only his sense of charity prevented him from cutting loose us ne'er-do-wells into a world where we would surely starve.

As I speak about Ebb and my dad and the small-businessmen of their generation, you may get the impression that I didn't learn much from them, or, if I did, that I don't acknowledge it. But that's not true. I learned a lot about many of the essentials of business from these old school guys. Never welsh on a debt. Always repay a favor. Don't blow your wad on fancy offices. Good old-fashioned rules that have been a guiding light to me in building 1-800-FLOWERS.

But good management? Forget it. In fact, I think you could write a whole book on the principles of bad management from those guys.

## The Seven Commandments of Bad Management

1. Never give a compliment—it gives the employees a big head.
2. Don't have a sense of humor—if people are having a good time, it means they are not getting any work done.
3. Don't look to develop people from within—hell, if someone starts as a clerk, they'll never change or grow.
4. Don't believe that anyone can have an idea other than you—if your employees know more than you, then why aren't they the boss?
5. Never criticize in private. When people screw up, make sure there are a lot of people around when you unload. It really puts the fear of God into everybody, kind of like a public execution. It may not raise morale, but it will make everyone really concentrate on covering their collective asses at all times.
6. Never apologize. If you are wrong, that's bad enough. Acknowledging it in front of your employees could breed disrespect and insubordination. Much better to try and blame mistakes on somebody else, especially if that someone else can't get back at you.
7. Never share information—very important. Anything the employees know about the business will either scare them, make them want more money, or end up in the possession of your competitors.

# BACK TO THE CASH REGISTER LOTTERY

In spite of Ebb's effort, we figured out a way to get a total picture of the business as well as an accurate ranking of everybody's sales performance. Ebb had one of those precomputer-era electronic cash registers. It had a little window you could peek through and see the sales slips as they accumulated. We came up with a system where each salesman would initial his own copies of the sales slips and put them in a box beside the register. That way, we could keep track of total sales and also of what was selling and who was selling it. Bottom line, we were able to keep score as we went along, and our natural competitiveness took over.

Selling became a game that each of us wanted to win. As with the refrigerator door, injecting fun into the workplace raised the level of camaraderie and, most important, productivity. Thirty years after I left Dadson's and our little betting parlor, I bet two people heading our interactive division that they could not meet a high sales goal before Christmas. They won. I lost. So the company sent a limousine to pick up Sharon and Donna and their beaus; it took them to Manhattan for dinner and a show, *The Starlight Express*. They all had a great time, and word spread through the company. I make a lot more bets now and lose most of them happily to a staff engaged in healthy competition that advances the company.

Competition only works if you keep score. Do you honestly think anyone would play golf if there were no score? You walk around and hit a ball, not very well, and then walk some more. Without a score there is no game. If you can find ways to keep score in business, two things will happen:

1. You will be able to quantify, which means more information, which means the ability to make better, more informed decisions.
2. Scoring enhances competition and provides standards against which we can measure performance. After all, you can't ask people to do better if you don't have some standard that says, "This is better and this is worse."

Having a means to measure and thereby set goals is a great way to motivate, but like any other business tool, it must be used properly to get the most out of it. Think of a typical sales meeting. The stage has a big banner emblazoned with a completely forgettable motto like "Winners succeed to excellence!" To the accompaniment of lasers and the *Star Wars* theme, some gasbag from senior management comes out and thunders, "This year we are going to exceed last year's performance by a hundred-and-ten percent!"

The applause doesn't quite rock the house. Why? After all, a goal of 110-percent growth should mean great prosperity for the company and its employees. The problem is, it is not a real number to anyone. But break it down to one percent a week and tie it to a compensation scheme and you have a tool that will spur performance and that you can use, if you just give it a little creative thought, to create competition. It is not enough to be in possession of the facts: you must present them in a way that communicates and motivates.

## Chapter Five

# The Contact Economy

At Dadson's, my fellow workers and I developed a sense of fun and competition. It brought us together and made us more productive. This lesson stayed with me when I went to college—an experience where, at the time, I thought I gained very little (my fault, not the college's). However, there was one psychology course that helped me give shape and form to the principles of human dynamics that I had learned on a gut level all through my life: at Dadson's, on the job with my dad, with Dave the milkman back in Grandma's kitchen. It is a concept basic to a school of psychology formulated in the 1930s by Claude Steiner. The academic name is transactional analysis, but the real crux of the matter was the notion of the stroke economy; for me, the contact economy.

According to Steiner, the thing that human beings crave most—more than success, or wealth, or fame—is social intimacy: contact. We all have a need to interact with other human beings. Taking this a step further, any positive human contact—a hug, a smile, a compliment, a word of praise—fulfills as fundamental a need as food or even sex. We crave those things that he called "strokes," and we all respond to them. They are the basic currency of our emotional lives, and try as we might to be creatures of the head and not the heart, they affect us powerfully. Convince someone mentally and you make a sale. Reach that same person emotionally and you have a customer who will keep coming back.

## FIRST CONNECT, THEN DO SOMETHING

It all came together for me at the group home in Far Rockaway. Making contact at the St. John's Home for Boys was not like going to a coed mixer at Princeton and introducing yourself to a shy English lit major from Indiana. These were street-tough city kids who had grown such a thick protective shield of character armor that no one could reach them. But I had to in order to survive in my job. One of the toughest nuts for me to crack was Joe.

Do you remember the movie *Stripes* starring Bill Murray? In it there was a character, Francis, who would kill you if you touched him. I think Joe could have been the model for Francis. Joe came from a terrible background that made him ripe for the penitentiary. Joe had no interests and no aptitude that I could detect. Actually, there was one thing he cared about: his hair. Joe had a thick head of black hair that was coiffed just so. He would look in the mirror and consider how to place a particular lock of hair in the precise perfect position, as if he were a painter laboring over a great portrait.

If you touched Joe, he would attack. If you touched his hair, he would go ape and try to kill you with his own two hands. He had an "I don't need anybody" attitude. People didn't like Joe. They left him alone and stayed out of his way.

Everyone except me.

I knew that leaving Joe alone would drive him further into his shell. In order to do any good with Joe I would have to find a way to get to him. Talking didn't seem to work, so— with some coaching from Bob Farrell—I made a point of accidentally on purpose bumping him in the halls. This was so out of the ordinary in an environment where everyone gave Joe a wide berth that it flustered him. Here I was, the authority figure, stooping to the level of horseplay! Joe became too puzzled to go into attack-dog mode. He actually liked the attention, which is what I was betting on. Simple schoolyard jostling gave Joe and me something in common, a way of communication that was just ours. If his father had given two licks about him, it's the kind of horsing around they would have done together. It got so that Joe started to expect a shove or a bump from me to make his day complete.

After this had gone on for a few weeks, I took the next step. I actually mussed up his hair and lived to tell about it! I knew then I was over the critical first hurdle, the same hurdle that you must clear in any situation involving two or more human beings: we were in contact on an emotional level and we had a medium of exchange. Next, it was up to me to see what I could buy with the emotional capital that I had built up.

# THE OLD TOM SAWYER TRICK

If you are the parent of teenage boys, you know that there is one inescapable truth about them. They eat like horses. With my own eyes I have seen my son Jimmy eat two double cheeseburgers, a large milkshake, an order of fries, and a half-eaten slice of pizza that his sister had left on the plate. When you take a bunch of teenage weightlifters and football players from deprived backgrounds—which accurately describes my group of boys at the St. John's Home—you are facing, grocery-billwise, the proverbial bottomless pit.

It didn't matter how much food I bought at the beginning of the week. Within two days, it was basically gone except for the canned corn and the frozen broccoli. We needed a storeroom, a *locked* storeroom. I decided to build it myself. Although my wife is unaware of it—and I trust you to keep it a secret—having grown up in a small contracting business, I actually do know how to use a hammer and nails.

So without talking to anybody, I brought in some lumber and my tools and started framing in a storeroom in the basement. One afternoon, Joe must have been missing his four o'clock hair mussing and, curious about the banging going on in the basement, he wandered in with Tony and asked what was up.

Tony was a muscular kid who had some emotional problems. Like a lot of troubled kids, though, he was able to mask it and somehow muddle through without the right people catching on. Tony's main problem was his temper. When he let it take over or, more accurately, when it overcame him, he was like an infant possessed by uncontrollable rage. Up to that point, Tony and I had never found a way to bond.

Joe and Tony showed up in the basement and were very curious about what I was doing. When I told them, they offered to help.

"Oh no, I don't think I could let you do that," I deadpanned. "I mean I'm not licensed to let underage kids use my tools." Like Tom Sawyer whitewashing the fence, I knew these kids wanted in on my project in the worst way.

"Aw c'mon, Mister Jim," they whined, not unlike the whine that any parent will recognize as the universal "we promise we'll do our homework if you just let us do this one thing."

"You'll do your homework?"

"All our homework."

"Well," I said, "it's kind of against the rules, but if you won't tell anybody, then I guess it won't do any harm."

So Joe got to use my power saw, not even minding if it blew sawdust on his hair. And Tony got to whale away with a hammer and nail. I got my storeroom—although Joe and Tony thought of it as "their" storeroom. When I put a padlock on it, I knew that any self-respecting kid from the projects could have it off in a New York minute, but I also knew that Joe and Tony had a proprietary interest in it. They were a team with equity in "the business." They would have punched the lights out of anybody who broke into their storeroom, something that I wasn't allowed to do in my position as a professional supervisor.

I got my storeroom. I built a team. They bought into my program. Every boy in the group home required a different approach, but my objective was always the same: find a basis for emotional contact. My no-win situation at St. John's was changing, and it was changing me.

## THE RIGHT CROSS AS AN EDUCATIONAL SYSTEM

As big, tough kids go, Bill and Ernie were the biggest and toughest that I ran into at the St. John's Home. One was a defensive end and one was a middle linebacker on the Far Rockaway football team. They pretty much ruled the roost and I pretty much let them, because I didn't have much of a choice.

One night we were shooting the breeze and Ernie asked, "Mister Jim, did you ever go camping?"

"Oh, yeah, sure," I said. "All the time." Which was a complete lie, but I figured I had to say something to preserve the golden opportunity of an actual conversation with these two.

"Well, why don't you take us camping?" one of them said.

"How much are you going to pay me?" I asked.

"Huh?" they said in one voice. (Actually, it was more like, "Pay you? What the ?*#!!@@!")

"You heard me. I work here on weekdays, not week-ends. And it may surprise you to learn I actually get paid for doing this. Watching over you guys is not my idea of a fun hobby. So if you want me to give up my weekend you need to pay me."

As they started to look something between angry and depressed, I sprung my plan on them. "Well," I said as if an idea that I had been playing with for some time was just dawning on me, "I know you guys don't have jobs so you don't have money to pay me, but there is a way that you could pay."

"Keep talking," Ernie said.

"How I get rated in my job is by how well I do in getting you guys to school. And I'm not doing that well. Every morning it's the same old thing. I run around and knock on doors and nobody listens." In fact, I usually was cursed at, threatened, and generally told to take a hike. "Perhaps you could motivate the other guys in the home to start getting to school. You know, they go to school, you get a camping trip."

Understand, when I say "motivate," Bill and Ernie had means at their disposal that I didn't—like they could kick the butt of anyone who didn't toe the line in a serious way. I especially needed help with José, with whom I struggled (and gave up) every day. José could curse equally well in Spanish and English and he let me have an awful earful.

I sprung the deal on them: "If everyone in this place goes to school for two solid weeks and no one cuts classes, I will personally buy the gear and take you guys camping."

I told them to set up a chart and keep a record, to mark off goals as they reached them. Bill and Ernie were totally jazzed by the plan and pretty soon everyone was checking the progress on the charts. We had a goal and a contract of sorts. And you should have seen what a little "encouragement" from Bill and Ernie did for school attendance.

The very first day, I went up and knocked on José's door and received the standard unflattering references to my mom. Nothing new here. So I went back downstairs and started to rustle up some breakfast. All of a sudden I heard a terrible *BAM!!* I ran upstairs. José's door had miraculously fallen off its hinges. Inside, Bill and Ernie were having a little "motivational chat" with José, who, you will have guessed by now, got to school on time that day.

Things were going well. Every day when the kids came back for dinner, Bill and Ernie were pumping iron and flexing their not inconsiderable muscles. When they paused to ask each kid if he had gone to school that day, the answer was always "yes."

By the time Thursday rolled around, the principal was wondering how to handle this sudden surge in school attendance. "And by the way," he added, "who the hell is José? He hasn't been here all year and all of a sudden he shows up four days in a row and I don't know what to do with him."

The chart kept filling in, the kids kept going to school. Bill and Ernie got their camping trip. And I managed to light a fire and keep everyone from getting eaten by the nonexistent timber wolves and grizzly bears of New York State.

I was interested in lighting a fire under a group of underachieving kids. You may want to motivate a company. But if your program hits the same points that we did in the Rockaways, you will have a blueprint for success. Not a guarantee, mind you: there is still such a thing as a market. However, every time I can check off these four goals, I know we have a fighting chance of succeeding. And we succeed a lot more than we fail.

- Set a goal.
- Measure every step of the way.
- Build in a performance bonus.
- Find a way to make it fun.

The fun, of course, is the glue that bonds people together and makes the other three targets that much more attainable.

## IT ISN'T JUST A NEW YORK THING

What was true for those kids in the Rockaways has also proven true at 1-800-FLOWERS and many other successful companies. To the extent that you connect to your people and connect them to one another, the windfall in productivity and spirit is enormous.

I have recently seen this in action at Gateway Computers, a company on whose board I have served. As many of you probably know, Gateway went from two brothers with a mail-order business in a barn to a six-billion-dollar-a-year computer hardware powerhouse.

The Gateway plant in North Sioux City, South Dakota, is mega: a bunch of nondescript low-rise industrial buildings spread out over acres and acres of fields. Not particularly interesting and no different from low-rise industrial mega-plexes anywhere in the world. The difference is Ted Waitt. Ted, with his ponytail and his motorcycle, is not your average coat-and-tie billionaire. In my youth, we would have said that Ted was a hippie.

I'm all for that. Anything that puts a little life and fun into the work situation is a plus. Last spring, when the corn was just sprouting and the Missouri River was still running up to its banks, everybody at Gateway came to work one Friday in their rattiest clothes. There were oil drums split in half and filled with charcoal. Burgers and hot dogs were grilling, sending up a mouth-watering aroma that was probably snif-fable all the way to Pittsburgh. Spray cans, paintbrushes, and rollers were handed out all around as the entire workforce—from exec VP down to assistant bubble pak packer—painted these enormous and boring industrial buildings in equally enormous black and white patches that looked just like the hide of a big dairy cow, which, as any computer nut will tell you, is the same fun packaging that sets Gateway computers apart from the other dweebish computer makers.

It was a real party. Paint fights, group pictures, and a chance to tweak the nose of one of the corporate big-wigs. Some people have no rhythm: this guy had no visual sense. You would have thought painting spots was a no-brainer. They were all outlined and all you had to do was paint inside the black line. Not Mr. Stanford Business Degree. He painted outside the line! I can't begin to estimate the amount of ribbing of the executive corps that this brought forth from the workforce.

Good!

The end result of the day was the whole Gateway company was energized. They had fun. They interacted. They smiled. Their brains discharged endorphins at a higher rate. Everyone made contact with everyone else on a new level. They connected. They have more of a relationship to the workplace, and on an emotional level, they "own" the paint job.

P.S.: Sales and production figures for the weeks following the paint-in were up.

## NOTHING CHANGES

The law of human relations that I learned in the St. John's Home, although it was years before I knew that I had learned it, is that doing business isn't first and foremost an economic activity. Yes, it is about economics and, yes, the consequences are measured in economic terms, but commodities do not buy and sell themselves. People buy them, sell them, make them. A product is part of a relationship. It is the thing that connects buyer and seller and producer. Therefore an entrepreneur who simply manages "things" will, in the long run, be at a competitive disadvantage to an entrepreneur who creates relationships among employees, customers, and vendors. The manager who perceives the workplace as an opportunity to have a good time as opposed to "doing time" will command more loyalty and be at the helm of a more efficient organization.

# MANAGEMENT SOFTWARE FROM THE HOOD

For me, the discovery of the value of relationships and the catalytic power of fun began by chance at the St. John's Home. The thing that was missing from those kids' lives was a relationship with a caring adult.

With the relationship established, the kids knew that I would be consistent and fair and, most of all, that I cared about them. I used many different approaches, but the end result was the same. From a relationship with me they were able to develop deeper relationships with one another and with our community of caring people at the home. It was not a big jump to transfer those lessons and skills to our company to create a culture where people feel connected, where they feel they can make mistakes as long as they are trying. I constantly look for ways to show them they are appreciated and to give them the best tools available for their jobs. They are encouraged to work in teams. Every manager is a coach. Every worker has a piece of themselves involved with the company. Customers sense this, and the web of relationships grows outward.

Good vibes are contagious.

## Chapter Six

# The Accidental Entrepreneur

## THE BUCKET SHOP

We all have a tendency to read our life history backward: we see the way things are today and then we look back to see the events that moved us down this path. Even though you may think that you and your mate were "born for each other," the truth of the matter might be that a missed train on one certain afternoon would have meant that at precisely 3:10 in the afternoon you wouldn't have been at the return counter at Macy's with the horrible tie with the palm trees on it that your aunt bought you for Christmas, which means you wouldn't have been on line ahead of that cute lady from the Bronx who laughed at you the more worked up you got with the stone-faced clerk, which made it harder and harder for you to stay mad. And if you then asked that lady out for a cup of coffee and fell in love with her and married her, a missed connection on the D train would have been a pretty big thing because without a reasonable on-time record from the New York City subway system, you might still be eating Cheerios over the sink and looking for the last clean sock in your bachelor pad.

Still, we look for the signposts to our future in the events of our past so that our lives make a nice three-act story just like a movie. In my case, I am sure my destiny in the flower business was sealed on one of my first real dates. It was with Margaret Sullivan. Actually, I don't know if it was my first time out with a girl, but it was probably the first time I went to the girl's house, met the parents, got the once-over from the dad, and then took the girl to a movie and an ice cream parlor.

Margaret Sullivan lived in Woodside, Queens. To get there I had to take the Q-10 bus up Lefferts Boulevard, get on the E or F train, then change for the Double-R at Roosevelt Avenue Station. There was a little flower shop in the Union Turnpike station, one of those storefronts that are known as bucket shops. Why are they called bucket shops? Because there was no room for a bathroom, so if you really had to go . . . Well, the flowers were all kept in buckets.

My friend Joe Juliano worked there so I stopped in on the way to Margaret's house to ask him to make up a bouquet of mums, carnations, and roses that cost me maybe $4 ($25 or $30 today).

Clutching my bouquet in my nervous teenage boy's death grip, I approached Margaret's door. I remember my hands were sweaty as I reached for her doorbell. Would she be happy to see me, or would she regret having said yes to such a nerd? Had she tried to reach me on the phone to tell me that she had come down with a twenty-four-hour broken leg?

As she opened the door, the first thing she saw was the bouquet that I was desperately trying to hide behind. Margaret broke into the biggest smile in the five boroughs. Next, she stunned me when she grabbed me real close and gave me a substantial kiss on the cheek. I remember stumbling backward and stifling an instinct to flee for my life.

Margaret saw the look on my face. "What's the matter?" she asked. "Did I do something wrong?"

"No," I said, making it up as I answered. "I'm—uh—uh—going to get more flowers."

As I look back, I think my future was sealed right there, even though it would be another ten years before I took the plunge into full-fledged entrepreneurship, or, more accurately, semi-fledged entrepreneurship.

## ON MY OWN

Within a few years of signing on as a live-in counselor at the St. John's Home, I applied for, and was given, the job of personnel director. It was one of the top jobs in an organization of nearly two hundred people. I went from making $12,000 a year to $18,000: a huge bump! If I had been following the usual Queens script, I was well on my way to a secure job and a pension. My grandmother predicted I might even do as well as another neighborhood college graduate who had gone to work for the sanitation department and with the aid of his degree, "moved right on up the ranks." Why, I could be out in twenty years, Grandma suggested, with $500 a month!

It wasn't enough. I wanted more out of life. I wanted to make more. I wanted more stimulation than I was getting on the old nine-to-five. I wanted to work for myself. This made me a budding entrepreneur, but at that point I didn't have any comprehension of what an entrepreneur was.

# TWO KINDS OF ENTREPRENEURS + ME

Of all the parts driving society's machine of wealth creation, the key is the entrepreneur, the person with an idea and the ability to turn that idea into an economic reality. When I was starting out on my own, there were, to my way of thinking, two kinds of entrepreneurs.

## 1. The Genetic Entrepreneur

Members of this species are born with a business-making chromosome. Where other kids set up a lemonade stand for a quarter a glass, this kid gives volume discounts on purchases over a quart, has a special lemonade and cookie package price, throws in a free comic book with purchase for every fifth customer, and often has a branch stand or two on the next block or at the exit from the schoolyard. He or she has eleven paper routes and half the kids in the neighborhood working for him. When this kind of entrepreneur grows up and has a business, a common behavioral trait is to stock up on free office supplies whenever he or she visits a lawyer or an accountant.

This is not an accurate description of me or my childhood, although it is pretty dead-on in regard to visits to my lawyer or accountant.

## 2. The Silver Spoon Entrepreneur

If you remember the TV show *Dobie Gillis*, there was a rich kid, Chadsworth Osborne Jr. Chadsworth had a chauffeur and a lunch box full of caviar. Life was handed to him on a platter. The silver spoon entrepreneur starts out like Chadsworth, although even he has to do something with what's on the platter to create more wealth. Usually, but not always, this species of entrepreneur goes to Harvard Biz. When he gets his first money-making idea, he writes a business plan, which he takes to his dad's friends, who are venture capitalists. They launch the business with a five-million-dollar initial funding requirement. He then does a mezzanine round of financing, which brings in another fifteen mill, which leads, within a couple of years, to an IPO and a big cash-out.

Before you knock this route, remember that Ted Turner and Howard Hughes, two of the great wealth creators of this century, each had a good family business as a base from which to build.

I am not a silver spoon entrepreneur, but I'll tell you what: in my next life I'm going to do everything I can to make sure that I am. It's a lot better than doing it all on your own with no money.

## JIM McCANN, ACCIDENTAL ENTREPRENEUR

By upbringing, education, and early track record, I fit neither profile. I dreamt of running a big business, but getting from point A to point B was a journey I had not yet mapped. I knew one thing: with my background, no one was going to hand me an opportunity. As a corollary to that, if I wanted an opportunity, I was going to have to create it myself. So, while keeping my job at St. John's (my motto has always been "Don't give up your day job!"), I started trying out second careers.

You begin by doing what you know. I knew how to fix up houses and make them look new, or at least desirably salable. So I started looking around for fixer-uppers. I would pick up houses cheap, get them in shape, rent them out, and finally sell them. It was money, but not what I wanted to do. For starters, I was required to put out ninety little brush fires all the time: leaky faucets, electrical fires, peeling paint, mildewed basements. I saw myself going down the same road that my father traveled: hand-to-mouth, chasing down customers, dealing with checks that bounced as high as a four-story walk-up. I wanted a business I could actually build and watch grow and enjoy.

As far as I had ever seen, a business was something that had a cash register, i.e., a retail business. So I knew I wanted to be in retail, but what kind of retail? A Burger King? A brushless disco car wash?

With a baloney sandwich in one hand, I began poring over the business classifieds during lunch hour at the home. I had my pick of failure-proof luncheonettes, Laundromats, and motels. This same section of the *New York Times* also carried franchises for sale.

A franchise sounded like a good way to enter the business world. By buying into a proven concept, it seemed to me, you lessened the risk as you leveraged off of someone else's knowledge. One day, early in my search, I came to an ad for a flower franchise called Flower World. I felt a tingle.

I liked the idea of flowers as a business. People are always getting married, having birthdays, graduating from high school, retiring, apologizing to girlfriends. Flowers and the customers for them are endlessly renewable resources. Given all that I had learned at St. John's about making emotional contact with people, the flower business interested me because it represented an industry built solely on the bedrock of the contact economy. Flowers were all about making connections with people, a human activity in which I firmly believed thanks to my career in social work.

*I love you!*
*Marry me!*
*Happy anniversary!*
*Happy birthday, Mom!*
*Welcome home, Grandma!*
*Thank you for having such a lousy serve in our tennis match!*

I was sure there was money to be made in flowers. In much the same way that the clothing business had come into the modern world back in the days when I worked at Dadson's, the flower business, which was still a very old-fashioned mom-and-pop business, was ready for change.

Years later, Brother Tom would remark that in my looking-for-a-franchise phase I had the look of a man driven. I was hell-bent on getting a franchise. "Lucky for you that the classifieds were alphabetical," Tom said, "otherwise you might have ended up with 1-800-XYLOPHONE."

# GOD WATCHES OUT FOR DRUNKS, SMALL CHILDREN, AND FIRST-TIME ENTREPRENEURS

Flower World was the brainchild of a visionary New Jersey florist named Bob Sheets. According to Bob, Flower World would create a national brand with stores that shared a look. They would all advertise in the Yellow Pages using the same design everywhere in the country. And—this sounded really good to me—they would offer twenty-four-hour-a-day customer service.

These were all good ideas, but even though Bob understood where the flower business was and where it could go, he did not have the necessary ability to execute. He did, however, have two sales guys with custom-made suits and impressive wood-paneled offices in the Seagrams Building on Park Avenue in New York City. They also had the world's slickest line of . . .

Suffice it to say, however, that Messrs. John Fiddes and Collins (gee, they had honest-sounding names!) had enough on the ball to sell a franchise to a twenty-five-year-old novice from Queens.

As they explained it to me, there was a franchise up and running that I could buy. It would not relieve me of the obligation to open up one new franchise as my entry fee into the Flower World organization, but it was already a going concern. Well, not exactly going, but it *could* go in the hands of a bright and energetic guy like me. The sales guys introduced me to Vic T.

Vic was a real character, a Greek-American in his thirties whose parents had owned a flower shop that he and his brother had taken over. But they'd had problems and lost that business, and Vic had opened up a store on his own.

That didn't bother me a lot. After all, I knew about how my father and his brothers had loused up a family business. Then, as I learned while driving around with Vic to check out some of his greenhouse suppliers, it turned out there was also a divorce involved.

"I made a little mistake and she overreacted," Vic said, speaking about his soon-to-be ex-wife (who was, for the record, a very beautiful woman). "I met this gorgeous blonde. She was tall and amazing looking."

"The blond beauty was the mistake, Vic?" I asked.

"No, the mistake happened one afternoon when my wife went shopping with her mother. She came home early and there we were in the living room without any clothes on."

"Vic," I commented, "I would be really hard-pressed to

find where it was exactly that your bride of seven months overreacted."

Vic had to unload the business. It was in a good neighborhood and handy to the high-rent district of the East Side. When those people bought flowers, they didn't chintz on the roses and orchids. Vic's needing to sell and my wanting to buy landed me in my first shop. Appropriately enough, given Vic's amorous lifestyle, the store was called the Hot House.

I maxed my credit cards, borrowed from my family, and raised $10,000, which bought me Vic's shop at First Avenue and 62nd Street, an old but rapidly disappearing Irish-Italian neighborhood where the likes of Jimmy Cagney and Whitey Ford had played stickball and grown to manhood.

I still needed to open up a franchise on my own if I wanted to be a full-fledged member of Flower World so, six months later, with my East Side store doing very well, I bought a second store out in Staten Island and put my sister Peggy in charge.

All through this time I kept my sideline in real estate and construction and continued to hold my day job at St. John's. In fact it was ten years before I left that job simply because I could no longer continue doing it while running a business that had grown to fourteen shops in New York. I was an entrepreneur—and a successful one—but it took a long time before I believed my success was going to last. I was like some bankers and stockbrokers I know who never give up their taxi license—just in case.

# GEE, IT LOOKED GOOD IN THE BROCHURE

Flower World *sounded* great. As it turned out, it was my first, but certainly not last, experience with a deal that appeared to be good but turned out to be less than promised. Do you remember Mel Brooks's movie *The Producers*? Zero Mostel plays a has-been, fly-by-night producer, Max Bialystok, who romances widows, haunts Alzheimer's wards, and flatters ugly heiresses as he tries to raise money for a musical. As the foundation of his scam he picks the absolute worst idea he can come up with, a musical called *Springtime for Hitler* that shows "the fun side" of the Third Reich. He counts on the play being such a loser that it will open and close, so all the backers will have to accept that the show didn't work and that they lost their money. Hey, no big thing, it happens all the time in show biz. But the cute part is that Max Bialystok sells 9,000 percent of the stock and hopes to pocket it all when the show goes down the toilet.

Flower World was straight out of the Max Bialystok school of deals. It was a poorly run company. They were going to do a lot for me, but it turned out that all they did was cost me money while delivering on maybe 10 percent of their promises. They were in it for the franchise fees, which were quite substantial in that they had sold twenty times more franchises than they opened!

So there I was, in hock for everything I owned. In fact,

since I basically owned nothing, I was in hock for a lot more than I owned. Worse, I was in a business that I hardly knew. Not exactly the way you want to start out in the world of entrepreneuring. A number of my fellow franchise purchasers wanted to sue the bejeezus out of Flower World, but I didn't see how that would do me a whole lot of good. The money was long gone. If we won a judgment, that wouldn't bring much relief in terms of making Flower World live up to its obligations. Even if they had wanted to, these guys didn't know the business and therefore couldn't have helped us.

Rather than trying to get even, I was much more interested in getting ahead. Sure, I had displayed bad judgment and they had displayed a severe ethics deficiency, but neither of those factors was going to feed my family or pay my mortgage. The lesson I learned right then and there, and which I never forgot, was not only should you not cry over spilt milk, you shouldn't cry over anything: business is full of mistakes and reverses. Forget about them and keep moving ahead. Every time you stop to recriminate, or waste good energy going after dishonest people or just plain old incompetent lamebrains, you are not paying attention to building your business. And one thing you can be sure of: while you are not pursuing the main chance, your competitors are.

Within a year, the law caught up with Flower World and gave us the option of getting out of our franchise deals. "In a heartbeat" is too slow a description of how fast I cut loose.

# SECOND CHANCES AND THE OAKLAND RAIDERS

First impressions count for a lot. In dealing with people in business I find this to be true almost all the time: you can tell fairly quickly if you like a person, if you feel trust, if the relationship can go somewhere. It is not simply a question of looking at a résumé. A good writer can turn a mediocre person into a star on a résumé. But looking someone in the eye, taking their measure, feeling a connection or the absence of one—these are experiences that no amount of gilding the lily of work history will change.

Act on your feelings. Trust your gut. It is right more often than it is wrong. That doesn't mean that each of us is the world's best judge of people. Far from it, but it does mean that your emotions and intuition are the best indicators of how you will interact with somebody. In this world of the contact economy where interaction is the heart of the matter, you cannot have a better guide to what will work for you.

I had this lesson driven home to me shortly after I bought the store in Manhattan. A guy came in off the street and said he was looking for a job as a driver. This was fine by me. We could always use a responsible driver. There was something direct and likable about Tommy D. I was interested. I said, "Tell me a little about yourself, where you come from, your work experience."

Tommy had worked for one of the old family florists on the upper East Side, just below Spanish Harlem. This was a good reference. He knew more about the business than I did.

Then came the rest of the story. Tommy had had several run-ins with the police. Still, I had an instinct about Tommy. I liked his honesty about his past. He also looked like a guy who really wanted a job.

I took a chance and hired him. Tommy just needed a break. When he got one, not only did he make good on it, but he has also put in two decades as a counselor helping the next generation of troubled kids.

As the Oakland Raiders discovered a long time ago, other people's castoffs, also known as retreads and rescue projects, can give you something that no hotshot rookie can bring to the table: they know the ins and outs of the business and they truly appreciate the value of a second chance.

Trust your gut.

## CHANGE PLANS, NOT BUSINESSES

Soon after unloading my franchise obligations I changed the name of the business to Flora Plenty, which was the name under which we operated until we became 1-800-FLOWERS. Although the Flower World gang never followed through on their great ideas, it didn't mean the ideas were faulty. Actually, they were quite good and were among the reasons that I had jumped into the flower game in the first place.

I immediately started to put some of those ideas into action. We did a lot more merchandising. We put extra effort into more exciting displays. We opened earlier and closed later than the competition. We had twenty-four-hour-a-day phone service. This last feature may conjure up a picture of a bank of telephone operators like you see in those *Time Magazine* ads on television.

"Hello! I'm Tracy," an attractive young gal in a headset says as she walks down what we are led to believe is the Time Inc. Worldwide Telecenter, "and our operators are standing by to take your call."

Well, we didn't have a Tracy, or a telecenter, or any bright-eyed operators waiting to take your call. More often we had Yours Truly in my shorts at three in the morning after putting in eight hours at St. John's and another full day after that tending to the flower business.

This is how I knew that I wanted to be in this business. If I didn't want it more than anything, I couldn't have done it. Which brings me to a good rule of thumb: if you are in your own start-up business and you find yourself too tired to put in eighteen-hour days and then be on call for the remaining six, maybe you should think about another business. If, on the other hand, you have picked the right business for you, then you will not even think you have a choice about putting in the extra time: you just do it. And it helps to have a supportive spouse who can take an order at 5 A.M. without sounding groggy. The adrenaline of a start-up plays a big role. So does the panic that sets in as you contemplate your creditors taking your home, your car, the money for your kids' school fees—everything.

One thing I had not planned on was becoming a street peddler. Street peddlers were the opposite of my vision of wealth-creating entrepreneurs. They sold hot dogs or knock-off Rolexes. Street peddling was 180 degrees from the profile an up-and-coming entrepreneur would want. And running a bunch of street peddlers? I ranked that no higher on the Big Business food chain than the job Fagin had in *Oliver Twist*, running a gang.

My street peddling phase had to do with holiday shopping patterns on Staten Island. Our shop was in a strip mall off the main drag, Richmond Avenue. This was a six-lane major artery that shoppers from New Jersey and Staten Island would use on their way to Brooklyn and Queens to avoid the one-way tolls on the Verrazano Narrows Bridge.

Much as ancient hunters would perch themselves at a river crossing during a game migration, a bunch of young flower peddlers would set up at key intersections of Hylan Boulevard. Our business suffered. These guys and gals were cleaning our clock.

I had no choice. I got heavily involved in street peddling. It was either that or watch my business take a major hit just when we were starting to get up and running. If the peddlers had their stands out on the avenue, I would set up a bigger one. Right at the biggest intersection with the longest traffic light, I parked a big truck with our logo emblazoned across it. Then we set up planks in back of the truck and big five-gallon buckets with huge sprays of flowers. Lo and behold, we did more business at the street stand than we did in our shop.

My self-image notwithstanding, street peddling turned out to be a great idea. Sure, it wouldn't last forever, and no, you couldn't run a long-term operation out of the back of a truck, but while the street peddling vogue lasted, we had peddlers working out of every shop that we opened. At one time we had thirty peddlers spread over the Bronx, Queens, and Staten Island. We gave them shopping carts and old baby carriages. We had contests. We would give prizes for peddlers who could unload slow-moving inventory, just like the pools we had at Dadson's for moving the last pair of pink Beatle boots. We didn't have the money to hire anyone to run the operation, so I drove from location to location with the backseat, the passenger seat, and the trunk full of bouquets and buckets. I looked like the flower car at a Mafia funeral, although instead of a big black Cadillac I bombed around in a used Chevy Impala that I bought from Brother Tom at St. John's.

This episode, in addition to nearly dropping me from exhaustion, also taught me the importance of going with the business flow instead of rigidly following a preconceived notion of what your business is going to look like. Furthermore, it revealed a precept that I would follow as we moved into the electronic marketplace, first with telemarketing and then with internet commerce: *if the customers are not coming to you, then you must go to the customers.* Which is exactly what I did when I heard about a company called 1-800-FLOWERS.

## Chapter Seven

# Thank God I Was Stupid (Again!)

Between the morning I plunked down $10,000 for my first franchise and the afternoon when I paid millions for 1-800-FLOWERS, the story is one of ten years of growth from a *small* small business to a *big* small business. If it had ended there, you wouldn't be reading this book. Financially, I would have been very comfortable. By 1983, the year my brother Chris joined us full-time, we had grown to fourteen shops in the New York area and were, as far as I am aware, the only twenty-four-hour full-service florist chain in the nation. Eventually, I would have left my job at St. John's, although I lived off those paychecks as I took the profits from one shop and invested them in the next.

Chris, in addition to being my brother, is my reality check. Every fast-growing business needs one. No matter how big we grow, he knows and I know that we are still at heart two kids from Our Lady of Perpetual Help. I will admit that there are times that success can turn your head and increase your opinion of yourself. The bigger your company gets, the more you are surrounded by employees, suppliers, and PR people who have a vested interest in pleasing you. You might even start to believe some of the saintly things that are being said about you. When that happens, find yourself a Chris and remember, *none of us is as good as our PR.*

## KEEPING THE BUSINESS AFLOAT

Chris was fourteen years old when he started to help out at Flora Plenty. At that time, we used a storage space out in Queens that shared a cellar with all the stores on the block, one of which happened to be a high-volume Chinese restaurant.

One night there was a flood in the basement. Chris and I went to check it out. It was an unbelievably slimy mess. A kitty litter box for Jabba the Hutt comes to mind. Floating fish heads, egg roll fixings, boiled vegetables, soy sauce, restroom overflow. Chris and I laid some planks across the growing garbage pond and tried to rescue a few of our flowers. Then Chris lost his balance and went into the soup. He was so funky smelling that I stuck him in the back of the car and made him sit on a plastic drop cloth. When we got home,

Chris stripped down and I hosed him off in the backyard and we threw his clothes away.

I still keep a take-out menu from that restaurant in my drawer as a reminder not of how far the McCann brothers have come in this world, but of who we really are. Anytime one of us starts to act a little swellheaded, all the other brother has to do is say, "Feel like some Chinese food?" and we come back down to earth with a smile.

# THE MIRROR DOESN'T LIE

I remember exactly where I was the first time I heard about 1-800-FLOWERS. It was 7:14 on the morning of November 6, 1984. I had just stepped out of the shower and was shaving (back in a rare unbearded period). I was up to that critical part in the shave when you purse your lips, and squoonch them to one side as you try to bloodlessly trim your upper lip. I had the radio on and some fast-talking announcer was extolling the virtues of a nationwide florist service called 1-800-FLOWERS.

I was stunned. A company whose name was the same as its phone number. What a concept! I got the hugest tingle I have ever felt in the presence of a brilliant business concept. I have a clear, physical memory of continuing to shave with my face all contorted while my image in the mirror did a double take and turned to the real me and said—

*"McCann, that is the greatest idea you have ever heard. Do something about it!"*

# AN IDEA WHOSE
# TIME HAD COME

Even before I heard about 1-800-FLOWERS, I was already doing extensive telemarketing through our chain of fourteen stores. On a daily basis, I was learning what a potent tool it had become in the mid-eighties. Companies like Lands' End and L.L. Bean were already using 800-number technology to fill the gap created by the demise of the big department stores.

This trend in retail, the decline of the old stores, has long been laid at the door of the concurrent decline of the inner city as a retail center. I don't agree. As the consumers moved out to the suburbs, so did the big department stores. The prime shopping segment of the market would have been content to patronize those old-line department stores with which they already had a relationship. Those stores had the advantage of tremendous brand loyalty, but apparently they did not realize that their most precious asset was their customers. In much the same way as the leveraged buyout sharpies of the mid-eighties made billions by cannibalizing the undervalued assets of target companies, the new age telemarketing retailers made inroads by seizing the opportunity to capture another critical, and often undervalued, retail asset: the customer base.

I don't want to imply that the people running the department stores were idiots and that I would have done better. Although I think I would have recognized the importance of holding on to customers, it is always easy to figure out what you should have done once the whole situation has played out and all the facts are in. What really happened was that retail stores were more or less blindsided by telemarketing. As far as they were concerned, the *real* problem was the discount stores that were creeping into their margins, taking away their customers. In an effort to cut their expenses they eliminated much of the service and in-store amenities that differentiated them in the first place. At the end of the day, if you offer nothing more in terms of the shopping experience than the discount stores do, and if no matter how hard you try, you are still more expensive, can you give me one good reason why customers should continue to patronize your department store? Oh, yeah, you're a nice person: that should do it.

While the old-line retailers were fighting the discount barbarians at the gates, they missed the storm brewing over the horizon. Like a hurricane that gathers force way out in the Atlantic where no one is around to feel its effects, telemarketing was readying a long-distance assault on the old stores: Lands' End and L.L. Bean, to name two companies, realized that direct marketing now had efficient telephone technology at its disposal and that consumer use of credit cards had reached critical mass. Why hassle schlepping to the downtown stores or the jammed parking lots at the crowded malls when all you had to do was pick up your phone, dial a free number, and give the nice person your credit card number—all during the commercial break on *Eight Is Enough?*

I thought all this as I stood with my razor in my hand and the water continued to run. I had to get in touch with 1-800-FLOWERS. I wanted to be part of them.

## THERE IS NO SUPERMAN

Here is a piece of advice that comes from experience: don't do what I did. The fact that I am alive and still married after the first ten years of working all the time speaks more about my good luck than my good sense. All through the growth of our chain of flower stores, I continued at St. John's. Businesses could come and go, but a job with an institution—the church, the police force, the electric company—was good for life. Although I was a classic entrepreneur in almost every sense of the word, I still hadn't learned to completely cut loose and let the winds of risk fill my sails.

I joined up with 1-800-FLOWERS as a fulfilling florist: they took the orders; we at Flora Plenty fulfilled them and paid 1-800-FLOWERS a commission. Our orders increased dramatically. My workload started to redline. I would stop by our stores each morning and pick up the previous day's receipts, which were squirreled away in their "secret" hiding places. Then, looking like the accountant for a numbers running operation, I would show up for work at St. John's with a briefcase full of money and cash receipts, which I would reconcile during lunch. I wouldn't finish my St. John's work until eight or nine, which left me with a few more hours of bookkeeping for the flower business. I knew if I went home I would crash, so I would stay at my desk eating junk food and doing the books until 11:30, at which point I would drag my butt home, flop into bed, and start the whole grind all over again.

Something had to give. When a budget crunch hit St. John's I offered to become a part-timer. Soon after, I left St. John's for good. The flower business, with its new tele-marketing traffic, required my full attention. I would learn to ride on the energy of the extra adrenaline rush that an entre-preneur gets from working without a net. Buying 1-800-FLOWERS would teach me that, but I still had a way to go before life taught me how the entrepreneur game is really played in the big leagues.

## IF YOU CAN'T BEAT 'EM, BUY 'EM

At first, 1-800-FLOWERS was great for our business. After a year, however, there were some disturbing warning signs. The orders started to fall off. We began to hear rumors of financial trouble. Maybe they needed more working capital. And maybe I could buy a piece of an idea that I still believed in very much.

I got on a plane and went to Dallas, a city that I knew only through the TV show. Given my intimate knowledge of J.R.'s world, I wasn't too surprised when the 1-800-FLOWERS offices turned out to be as big as the Pentagon, or so they seemed. Fifty-five thousand square feet, rows of hard-wood desks, people in suspenders and British shirts as if they were running Merrill Lynch. Only problem was, they weren't

Merrill Lynch and they were losing a fortune. They had caught the eighties disease: pride. Or, more properly, COR-PORATE PRIDE—and along with it, its nearly always mortal symptom, KILLER OVERHEAD.

## WHAT'S WRONG WITH THIS PICTURE?

Remember what I said about the danger of a successful businessperson believing the line the PR folks are handing to the rest of the world? This goes double for businesses that are started with a lot of fanfare and a staff of high-priced hotshots. I am reminded of the reaction I have when I go to see a really bad show or movie with big stars in it. What could they have possibly been thinking about when they made *Judge Dred* or *The Postman?*

What happened was someone sold the idea really hard. That next person then sold it really hard to a decision-making group. Then the internal communications people started beating the drum within the company about a hot new property. Then for whatever reason—call it vanity or just plain old bad advice—a big star signed. The ball kept rolling downhill picking up momentum. Surely, you would think, someone would have latched onto what a stinker was in the works once there were some scenes to look at. But no, by that time everyone was so invested in the project's success that they saw only what they wanted to see.

I think the same thing happened with many overhyped

new companies back then. One hell of a salesperson put pencil to paper and wrote a whale of a prospectus. It was the eighties. There was no such thing as a bad deal, especially in Texas where real estate and oil were as hot as they could be.

The original 1-800-FLOWERS group raised $20 million. Actually, it may have been more than that. I know they *spent* something like $30 million in the first year. They built the world's biggest telemarketing center. They had million-dollar telephone switches and equally pricey state-of-the-art IBM computer systems. They had a bridge for their command post that was straight out of the twenty-first century. They had 700 workstations, all mahogany, for a business whose only contact with customers was on the telephone. They had 120 managers and two Ph.D.s with degrees in education and training on payroll before they had any sales staff to train or manage! They hired Chiat Day, which was at that time the hottest ad agency in the world (recall the famous Macintosh Superbowl ad), to turn out clever, gorgeous ads. They did nationwide market tests. They had Merrill Lynch behind them. In a word, they appeared to have *everything*.

## WHAT'S THE OPPOSITE OF A GUSHER?

With all that horsepower behind it, how could they miss? Easy. Do you have any idea what kind of numbers you have to do to service a debt of $15 million? Well, $15 million in debt at 10 percent is roughly $125K per month in interest before you even turn on the lights! And once they started spending money, they had to spend more money just to catch up with the momentum they had generated. They dropped a million dollars on a creative campaign prior to an equally pricey test launch. When the test launch proved that their projections were way too rosy, did they pull back and regroup? No way! Thanksgiving, Christmas, Valentine's, Easter, Mother's Day were hard upon them, and if they didn't start to generate some income during these six critical holidays—during which many florists do nearly half of their business—then they could kiss another year good-bye. At the rate they were spending money, they couldn't buy another year, so in spite of the test results they prayed and launched nationwide.

The beginning news was good: 6,800 fulfilling florists (our company among them), lots of orders, lots of ads. On the downside, 800 numbers were still new to most consumers and it was going to take time to build their confidence in a new long-distance supplier. Beyond that, it would have taken more money than anyone could have hoped for to offset the tremendous outlay and debt to that point. The business model wasn't working.

That's when the ads disappeared. And then the orders started to decline. I wrote a few letters that had zero effect. I had to do something so I hopped on the next plane to Dallas to offer help. Long story short: they didn't particularly care about my money. They wanted me to run the company! They didn't want to appear to the world as people who had made a turkey investment.

# AN ENTREPRENEURIAL SHORTFALL

What followed were two years of infuriatingly slow, undirected negotiations. Lots of people were involved, and they all had different agendas. You see, although 1-800-FLOWERS was a troubled business with an unrealistic business plan, the original investors were not bad businessmen. In fact, quite the opposite. Taken individually they were very talented, successful, and, in some cases, brilliant people. The problem was, as one of them later explained to me, "None of us had a ham sandwich in this deal." In other words, 1-800-FLOWERS was small potatoes given the nosedive that oil and Texas real estate were taking. Their family fortunes were threatened. In that scheme of things, the fate of a side investment in the flower business didn't amount to a very large hill of pinto beans. The investors were quite content to let the hired management go along and make a series of bad decisions.

As I look back on it, I think the big mistake was that there was no one among the original investors who had an entrepreneurial stake in the business, nobody who lived and breathed it, nobody who said, "This is my baby." The investor group had much bigger fish to fry. This deal had "write-off" written all over it. Well, not to me. What seemed like a pisher deal to them looked like the opportunity of a lifetime to me. There was one person who would live, eat, and breathe 1-800-FLOWERS, and that was me. I hung on to that deal like a bad cold that wouldn't go away.

As the second year of this dance was going on, I was in Orlando at Disney World with my family on our first vacation in many years. (Did you ever notice how often people tell you that they haven't taken a vacation in ten years? If even half of those stories were true there would be no Disney World, no Club Med, no Hertz. In my case, however, this was the case. Ten years, no vacation.) I remember talking to my wife at that point and asking what I was doing wrong. I had, by that time, logged no fewer than twenty-five coach fare tickets on Braniff (coach because I didn't want to waste the money on first class and Braniff because they had the cheapest fares to Texas). I rented a small car, ate in the motel coffee shop, and spent eighteen dollars for a room. But the 1-800-FLOWERS boys would pick me up in a fancy car and we'd dine at the best restaurant in town.

## I HAD ME OVER A BARREL

They were losing a bloody fortune and still enjoying the expense account lifestyle (in some ways I think the crash of '87 was nature's way of telling us to mind our expense accounts). As things turned out, I am very lucky to have made that deal and bought the company, but going in, it was a pretty lousy deal for us. If I had known more, I wouldn't have done it—call it my own "due negligence." But I was a small businessman, not an eighties deal guy. My family lawyer—who was great at looking over wills or New York real estate—advised me, and he was almost as clueless as I was in this world of arbitrageurs and deal guys. Honestly, at that time in my life, I didn't really know what an investment banker did!

But I did know a thing or two about making money and building a business. Although we were by no means a *Fortune* 500 (or even *Fortune* 5000) company, our fourteen flower shops were very successful, and we did have cash to spend. Not enough cash to fund the original scope of the 1-800-FLOWERS business plan, but enough to be talking seriously about our plan. It was right about then that a phone call that I received in Disney World became the final element that clinched our deal for 1-800-FLOWERS.

It was Jim Poage on the other line, one of the two very successful businesspeople from Dallas who had put together the original investor group. He cut right to the chase.

"I have been negotiating this deal with you for a few months, and the thing that has impressed me is your passion for the idea. That is something we were always missing. I see your plan, and I think it is really exciting. It's what I had hoped for from 1-800-FLOWERS in the first place, but we weren't able to execute properly. Don't know why. I'm not blaming, but it just didn't happen."

Meanwhile, there I am in my running shorts in a hotel near Disney World trying to figure out if we want to have crêpes suzette at the French Pavillion or visit Epcot, which was, in my mind, a modernized knockoff of the 1964 World's Fair in Flushing. So there I was flipping a coin between crêpes and waffles listening to Jim Poage teeing-up my future. I didn't really grasp where he was coming from, so I did something that was very untypical of me. I kept quiet while Jim continued.

"If you are interested, I would like to switch sides and come in as your partner, because I share your passion and I think you are the guy to make it happen. What I am saying is I am willing to throw in a pile of money alongside yours."

I was shocked, elated, flabbergasted; but, as it turned out, Jim Poage was serious, and within a few months, my two years of negotiations ended with Jim Poage and me in possession of all the worldly goods and out-of-this-world debts of 1-800-FLOWERS.

The nuts and bolts of the arrangement were that Jim Poage and I put in millions and assumed millions more in debt, along with all the future obligations of the company. In return we inherited forty boxes of useless records and a phone number. We didn't even inherit the phones, because no sooner had we bought the company than our service was cut off and we were booted out of our office in Texas. I was millions in debt, leveraged up to my eyeballs. The first sign of my new big shot status was that within days of the purchase, my brother and I were crawling around with wire cutters and screwdrivers, calling on summer job knowledge from our youth to install new phones. And then it was up to the two of us to answer the phones until we hired some help.

Now that I have an opportunity to move in the world of major businesspeople I am often asked, "Instead of trying to climb out of the hole, why didn't you just go Chapter Eleven?"

First off, I didn't know how to do it. It had never been an option in the world I came from. When I was a kid, there was very little distinction between bankruptcy and suicide. Come to think of it, the few times I did hear the word, it often was by way of explaining a suicide. Furthermore, going bankrupt would have left a lot of creditors—florists just like me, with small businesses and growing families—out in the cold. From beyond her grave, Margaret McCann would have wagged her finger at me and said, "Shame on you, Jimmy!"

I had buried myself in debt and I was going to have to climb out of it or sink, but I wasn't going to take the small shop owners in the flower business down with me. So within a week of becoming the proprietor of the far-flung, thoroughly debt-ridden 1-800-FLOWERS "empire" there I was, on the phone, at a makeshift desk composed of planks and packing crates, working the hold buttons. "Thank you for calling 1-800-FLOWERS, this is Jim speaking. How can we help you today?"

## A NEW YORK STATE OF MIND

While I was down in Dallas, learning to talk like a good ol' boy, I was reminded that I came from a different world. I received a call from Lucy Estefan telling me that we had been robbed. If you are a small retailer in New York, you learn to think of robbery the way retailers in Los Angeles look at earthquakes: not pleasant, potentially dangerous, but they come with the territory.

"Anybody hurt?" I asked.

"No."

"Was it a lot of money?"

"No money."

I was in the dark: getting stuck up for no money did not compute from my experience of robbers. It turned out we had been hit at one of our stores that had formerly been a Brooklyn bank. There were big, thick, impressive doors of metal and glass. Over the years, the doors had gotten a little out of plumb and needed some attention. The repairmen came in their truck and fiddled with the doors for about twenty minutes, at which point the foreman came in to tell our store manager that the doors needed to be taken down to his shop for some major work. So they took the doors away. Seven hours went by; our manager needed it back so he could close down for the night. He called the door repair company and the repairman had never returned. We had been doorjacked!

I don't know what he was thinking about or how he thought he was going to unload the doors. They weren't the kind of thing you could hide under your overcoat as you approached people on the street—"Psst, want to see some nice doors?"

## Chapter Eight

# A World-Beating Idea

Although there were many people—make that everybody but me—who had serious reservations about going in hock to buy 1-800-FLOWERS, I still thought the 800 number concept was brilliant. This belief comforted me on the endless trips I took to Dallas in the months right after the purchase. On one of those trips I found myself in conversation with a Texas businessman who spoke with a silky smooth Lone Star accent. Both of us had decided to forego the inflight movie (the always riveting *Ice Castles*) so we fell into a conversation about families and businesses. When he asked what I did for a living, I told him I had a nationwide florist business.

"What's the name of your company?" he asked.

"800-FLOWERS," I said proudly, noticing a puzzled look coming across my planemate's face.

"Why 800-FLOWERS? Why not 750-FLOWERS?"

"You know," I said to myself, "maybe this isn't as big an idea as I thought it was."

## CONVENIENCE ISN'T EVERYTHING

If people made buying choices according to a rational formula, 1-800-FLOWERS should have roared right out of the box. The sheer convenience of it seemed unchallengeable. Many people often have the thought, "Gee, maybe I should send some flowers." They have any number of reasons for wanting to send them—thank you, sorry, congratulations, etc. Flowers have always been given for just about any event in a person's life that involves a relationship—with a school, a job, a spouse, a kid, a mom. But between intending to send flowers and actually sending them there are all the other demands on your time and thoughts. For most people, most of the time, it's a big deal to make a special trip to the flower shop. And then, what do you do with the flowers between the time you buy them and the time you give them? And do you actually have time to make another trip to give the flowers? Nice thought, big hassle.

Our business offered extraordinary convenience. All it required was a telephone call of approximately two minutes. The world should have been beating a telephonic path to our telecenters. Of course, nothing is that easy, and pure logic is rarely enough to capture and keep customers. First you have to make them feel at ease. Next you want them to like you and, by extension, trust you. You can offer products but you have to earn trust and respect.

# RECOGNIZING THE CHALLENGE

Our immediate challenge at 1-800-FLOWERS was not, as you might expect, racking up sales by telephone. Sure, telephone commerce requires a product to buy and sell. Self-evidently, it also requires a person on one end of the line to sell—no problem there because I had phones, flowers, and nice people. Still, the most important part of the job is to "get people into the store." In our case it meant they needed to think of us when they had the urge to buy flowers and then they needed to pick up a phone and call us. *That* was the challenge.

Cute and easy to remember as the number 1-800-FLOWERS was, there were some built-in problems. First, 800 technology was rather new, more the exception than the rule. Was it reliable? Was it safe to give out your credit card number to a stranger? Wasn't a company that was just a phone number kind of remote and not part of your local world? Who could you yell at if things went wrong? Would it be just like dealing with the phone company? The post office?

All of these legitimate questions had to be answered before we could begin to unlock the potential customer base.

We went straight at our weak point: lack of proximity to the customer. First and foremost, we offered twenty-four-hour service. Anytime you wanted to buy flowers, anytime you had a problem or a question, one of our reps was there. Second, our reps were hired on the basis of their warmth and friendliness on the telephone. When you called us, you were guaranteed to be handled by someone who liked people, and who projected a credible feeling of wanting to satisfy, and who knew our product. I thought of the example of Wal-Mart, which is known as a very cost-conscious company. Every Wal-Mart always has a greeter to orient and welcome you whenever you walk into one of their stores: a person with a big smile and a big personality who creates a personal relationship with the customer at the very outset of the buy/sell event. Third, just like Nordstrom we offered a no-questions-asked refund policy. If you weren't happy, you got your money back. We took a negative—a sense that we were remote and long-distance—and we turned it into a positive: we are all over the country, we have thousands of people working with the freshest, most beautiful flowers, and all of them will use all of our enormous resources to make sure you are happy.

## TIFFANY'S MOST IMPORTANT PRODUCT: BLUE BOXES

Say that you are a valued employee and you have just given birth to your first child. It was a difficult pregnancy, but your baby, a strapping seven-pounder, was born healthy, hungry, and happy. Your boss is out of town but wants to do something special for you. Flowers would be great, but maybe the boss wants to do something even more special. He buys you some gorgeous silver earrings, little pear-shaped dangling earrings. He thinks you will like them. He has an idea to ensure that you know what a special gift it is. Instead of going down to the jeweler at the mall, he orders from a company that delivers the gift in a little blue box tied with a white ribbon. Before you even open the gift, you inhale appreciatively when you see the box. There could be an onion inside for all you know, but the message is very clear: "He cared enough to buy me Tiffany. That is very special."

Tiffany jewelry, nice as it is, is even more valuable and special because it is a special brand. Brands, as I have said before, are very much like celebrities in this day and age. We develop relationships with them. We will buy the product with a certain brand name in the same way we will go see any movie with a favorite actor or actress. Of course you need advertising to let people know you are out there and to remind them of you amidst the clutter of all the other advertisements for competing products (and I believe every other product is competing with me for your time). The most important thing I can do to maintain and increase my position in the market is to build a relationship and, taking it one step further, to make that relationship an equal partner with our product in establishing a brand identity.

# WORD OF MOUTH: STILL THE BEST ADVERTISING

One word of praise or recommendation from a satisfied customer is worth much more than even the slickest advertisement. A real person's testimonial to another real person has a tremendous ripple effect. Advertising is one of the most costly ways to capture a customer. Servicing customers, one individual at a time, is more cost-efficient, more enduring, and it makes a greater impact in creating a brand image.

So I am looking for a Vice President of Word of Mouth, someone who can take the thousands of personal success stories in our company and incorporate them into our brand image. If, as I have often said, flowers are a hyperlink to our emotions, then personal contact and service is the hyperlink to customer creation. If any problem comes down to a choice of doing it quickly and cheaply or taking more time to service a customer, the choice is always service. The word of mouth will do you good long after the roses have faded (they never "die").

# CHEERS FOR TEARS

In our business, Mother's Day, to coin a phrase, is "the mother of them all." If you are in the flower business and it's Mother's Day, it always seems, as one of our more colorful

Texas reps once explained to me, "your dogs are barking and you are plumb out of gas." My self-image on Mother's Day is of one of those little bouncy figures that people stick in the rear window of their cars. You know, the ones with a big Snoopy or Charlie Brown head that bounces empty-headedly as you tool down the highway. If anyone took a scan of my brain waves late in the afternoon on Mother's Day, I'm sure it would flatline.

It was about 6:00 in the evening on one Mother's Day when we received an order from a man who wanted to send flowers to his shut-in aunt at a nursing home outside town. Even though it was late, we asked our fulfilling florist if he could make the delivery.

"I'm out the door, anyway," he said. "I don't have any plans beyond a shower and sleep. No problem. What's the address?"

The florist closed up his shop and headed out to the nursing home. In the back seat, he had two bouquets, one for his own mother and one for Idela Smith at the home. When he arrived at his destination, he took the Smith bouquet and went up to the desk at the nursing home. In addition to the nurse on duty there was a little old lady with silvery white hair and a flower print dress—all dressed up with nowhere to go.

"Are those flowers for me?" she asked in a thin voice.

"Mrs. Smith?" he asked. "These are for Idela Smith."

Right then and there he saw that he had said the wrong thing. The little old lady's eyes welled up with tears. "No. I'm Mrs. Williams. My kids never remember me," she said with all the heartbreak that only a forgotten mother can summon up.

Feeling absolutely horrible, our sensitive florist went back to his car and sat in the front seat for a minute. He was majorly bummed. Then, he said to himself, "Mom will understand." He reached into the backseat and picked up the bouquet intended for his own mother. He didn't even have to change the message. "Dear Mom," it said, "You're the greatest." He went back into the nursing home and walked up to the sad old lady.

"Mrs. Williams, I have so many deliveries in my car, I must have missed yours. I'm terribly sorry, but here's a bouquet from the kids. Happy Mother's Day."

Mrs. Williams started to cry from happiness, and so did the nurse on duty and so did our florist. The whole place got into the act and had a great cry, just like a wedding on *Search For Tomorrow*.

That's what I call building word of mouth. If the florist had been a different kind of guy, if we hadn't been the kind of company that places a premium on people and making an emotional contact, it wouldn't have happened. The nice-guy points he racked up went right into our good karma account, where they helped define our brand.

## THE BRAGABILITY INDEX

When you were little, I am sure people told you, "Nobody likes a braggart." Although this is true in a personal sense, the business world plays by different rules. If you don't toot your own horn, who will? I am not talking about corporate cheerleading and going around saying, "We're number one" or "Eat our dust!" That's just posturing and better left to roosters than quality businesspeople. The kind of bragging I am talking about is stories that reveal the true nature of your company and the people working for it. If you have a story like "Mrs. Williams's Bouquet," you need to get it to your people, make it part of the culture of the company. You need to reward this kind of behavior. This sets a tone in the company, and guess what? All of a sudden, you will find that encouraging a certain kind of behavior has the effect of defining your corporate culture in the way you desire it. You can't control your company's culture. It exists, lives, and changes as if it is alive. You can, however, influence your company's culture. In fact, everything you do will influence it.

## THE COP AND THE ROSE

In addition to Mother's Day, the other holiday that tests our ability to the max is Valentine's Day. Everybody is in love with love on Valentine's Day, and wants to send flowers to prove it. I remember the year after "Mrs. Williams's Bouquet," I went looking in the telecenter for one of our supervisors, Gloria. She was busy and asked not to be disturbed. I went over to her workstation near the bridge and asked her what was up. As she told it, her last three hours had been taken up trying to get one order delivered to a customer's sickly great-aunt in a small town in the boonies outside Pittsburgh.

Gloria had tried to find a florist who could make the run, but it was just one of those things where there wasn't a florist in the area, because it was so remote. Instead of giving up, Gloria called the local policeman (also the owner of the hardware store), who said that the old woman actually lived near his uncle's farm. He offered to make the delivery. So Gloria had the bouquet delivered to the police department/hardware store, where it got a full escort out to the sick aunt.

The next day we got a call from the policeman, who had just received a call from the lady who received the flowers, who told him, "You didn't just make my day, or my week, or my month. You and my wonderful nephew made my whole year!"

An advertisement may get people to remember your name, but one story like "The Cop and the Rose" will hit home more deeply with people and bind them to your company for a long time.

Sure, having a senior supervisor blow three hours during one of the two busiest days of the year doesn't compute on the bottom line, but it is the kind of seed that, once planted, will yield sales and build customer relationships far in excess of anything Gloria could have sold or helped to sell in those three hours.

# A GREAT RESTAURANT'S SECRET

We try to satisfy every customer. We don't always succeed, but we try. In this age of the internet where everybody is electronically in contact with everybody else, a ticked-off customer can start flaming us all over the net. Remember, that same new medium that can work for you so powerfully also turns out to be a potent weapon when you mess up.

Our standard instruction for handling ticked-off customers is "Find out what it will take to make the unsatisfied customer happy, then do it." This is a maxim that any successful businessperson knows without being told, and it applies to all businesses where one deals with the public. Sirio Maccioni, the wildly successful restaurateur who created New York's top celebrity restaurant, Le Cirque, always calls any dissatisfied patron the next day to apologize. The customer may have been dead wrong and a loud drunk to boot, but Sirio offers his apologies and invites the aggrieved diner in for a glass of champagne or perhaps a complimentary meal. For twenty-three years, every pissed-off customer got a make-nice call from Sirio. The amount of business he has wooed back and kept is vastly impressive. He understood that the relationship part of the equation counted much more than the question of whether the meat was medium rare or medium well.

Basically I give the same advice to our customer satisfaction people. For the long-term health of our business, happy customers are as important as the average rainfall in the rose-growing valleys of Mexico or frost in the tulip fields of the Netherlands.

# THE EMERGENCY WARD

I was reminded of Sirio's supersmooth method one morning when I received a letter from a nurse at a big city hospital. She is a triage nurse, which means she has to decide which cases need immediate attention and who waits (either because they will survive if they wait or because they are not going to survive anyway so you might as well treat the people who have a chance).

This was obviously one tough lady, able to handle a lot of pressure. But she was also a human being, and couldn't help building up a lot of internal pressure because of her job. There came a time when she had to unload on someone, and our service rep, Barbara, caught the full brunt of the nurse's considerable reserves of anger.

As the triage nurse explained in her letter, she was furious that the very special flower arrangement she had ordered for her mother had never arrived. She was particularly galled—and let us know it—because she had devoted so much thought to the bouquet and had been so specific in her instructions.

Barbara listened politely all through the tirade and, when it was done, asked for the address again, the kinds of flowers, and the wording of the note. The very next day, she had the flowers delivered, on time, exactly the way the angry nurse specified. Barbara also sent the customer a handwritten note on plush, salmon-colored stationery: "I am sorry that you were upset, and I hope we will work this out."

Soon afterward, the nurse sent a thank-you note that virtually blushed with embarrassment. "What I didn't know," the nurse wrote to Barbara, "is that you knew all the time that the mistake was mine. I had given you my mother's old address!"

The customer was wrong, we were right, but we gained a customer for life, and piles of goodwill by not getting into who was right and who was wrong, but simply trying to satisfy the customer.

## THE CUSTOMER IS ALWAYS RIGHT

Wrong. But they are always the customer.

1-800-FLOWERS has an "absolute guarantee" policy that is unique in the floral industry. If, at any time, you are not satisfied with the product you ordered, we will replace it. Or refund your money. Or do whatever it takes to ensure that you, the customer, are happy and will continue to be a customer of ours in the future.

This policy has served us well. Some of our most loyal customers are people who originally had a minor complaint, but were then absolutely knocked out by what our customer service team did to correct the situation. We actually have a "Legends" book filled with stories of associates going the extra mile to please a customer. We give the Legends book to new associates when they ask, "What are the rules for working in customer service?" Our response is a simple one: "There are no rules. Just read this book. If what you do is not worthy of being included in the book, you probably haven't done enough."

Sometimes, though, doing enough is not enough. It doesn't happen often, but occasionally we get a customer who tries to take advantage of our customer service policy. These people complain no matter what. On the rare occasion when our records indicate that we have gotten multiple complaints from a person, we are drawn to the conclusion that we would be better off without this person as a customer.

This happens so rarely that it is practically a nonevent. But you know where the real value of this policy is? With our customer service associates.

They are hard-working people who spend their time making sure our customers are happy. It bothers them when they see someone trying to take advantage of their company. That's why we instituted a policy a few years ago whereby a select group of senior associates can determine when it is appropriate to ask a caller to take his business elsewhere. By allowing them to just say "no" to the occasional abusive customer, we have shown our support for their judgment.

And, ultimately, happy staff members make for happier customers.

# THE NEW CUSTOMER RULING CLASS

A reputation for service was a linchpin in the development of our brand identity. The customer knew we were accountable for our products. High-quality customer service puts our best practitioners of the contact economy into a relationship with customers. We tried to be the best at this by hiring better reps, training them to connect with the customer, and backing them up with an organization that regards service not as a pain but as a long-term relationship-building opportunity.

Today, more than at any other time I can think of, you must intrigue, please, and entertain the customer. They are the new ruling class in our consumer-oriented economy, and they have specific needs.

## 1. Give Me a Reason to Come to Your Store

In my youth, there were very predictable flower-buying times of the year. You could count on steady walk-in traffic during Easter, for example. The same principle operated in the clothing business. Kids went back to school in the beginning of September so clothes and shoe stores had a big spike at the end of August. Although we still see blips around certain times of the year, we don't see the all-or-nothing cycles that we had in the old days. People spread out their buying over the course of the year. Flowers are not just for special days anymore. They are for special people whenever we want to let them know we have a special feeling for them.

If you want to bring people to your store, you have to make it easy for them to get there, and you have to have something to add to the value proposition once they get there. Which leads me to the two critical components of our appeal to the New Customer Ruling Class.

## 2. Emphasize Service

Having just discussed this at length, I think you know how strongly I feel about service. It's the next most important thing after having a product to sell.

## 3. Be Accessible

In order to buy your goods or services, people need to be able to find you. Once upon a time that meant a good location for your store. It still does, but that is not enough. As I have said countless times, I bought 1-800-FLOWERS because I believed in the telemarketing revolution, and having a phone number that was also the name of the company was the telemarketing equivalent of having a store at the inter-section of the best business streets in town.

Having built our business largely through exploiting the technology of 800 numbers, we knew the value of electroni-cally assisted commerce. When the internet came along, it didn't take a whole lot of business acumen to figure out the potential for our company. As 800 technology was ten years ago, the internet is now: a lot of promise in a new and growing field. When people started to talk about the inter-net, we looked at our business and saw a true north heading on our cultural compass, so we fired up our modems and jumped on the net with a passion.

Now with hundreds of stores, a sophisticated and efficient telemarketing arm, a strong and profitable presence on the internet, and a number of catalogue offerings, anybody can reach us in any number of ways. It's easy to do business with us. Or, to paraphrase *Field of Dreams*: We built it so they (the customers) would come.

## 4. Let Us Entertain You

While you are out there trying to out-service, out-telemarket, and out-internet your competitors, they are probably doing the same thing. You just have to be smarter and better. You need to work harder. You also need to realize, as we explored in the New Retail Paradigm, that there is an evolving convergence between entertainment and commerce. You need to ask yourself, "What can I do in any customer encounter that will make it a more enjoyable experience?" In human contact terms, enjoyment is the equivalent of increased efficiency on the hardware and systems side of your business.

Recently we hit upon a way to combine entertainment with a new reason to come to our stores. We began to search out local artists in some of the towns where we have retail operations. Working through local arts organizations, we solicited submissions and after looking at a lot of terrific art, we selected one artist to exhibit in each of those stores. Next we printed up invitations and sent them out to arts supporters in each town—who, by the way, are usually among the leading citizens.

Then we had a bona fide art opening/cocktail reception. Our floral designers got involved and worked on arrangements that showed off the art to its best advantage. Everybody got dressed to the nines. For the artists, many of whom had never had a real showing, it was a great kick (and, since they made some sales as well, it also meant a nice check or two to walk away with). All we required of the artists was that they donate a percentage of their revenue to Very Special Arts, on whose board I serve. (Very Special Arts, founded by Jean Kennedy Smith, is an international nonprofit organization established to bring the arts to the disabled community.) These art openings brought a lot of the community leaders to our stores and connected us with the community in an ongoing way. I don't think I have to tell you that we started a lot of customer relationships at those openings.

## 5. Use Technology to Improve Quality

All over the world, technology, all technology (not simply information technology), is squeezing the inefficiencies out of every aspect of modern business. No matter how good your product is, no matter how efficient your organization, you don't have a choice about whether or not to embrace technology. Do it or close up shop before someone else cleans your clock.

You will make some good technology choices and some bad ones. The good ones will allow you to offer more features in your products and to do this in a more cost-efficient way. It will also help you to improve your quality, and quality goes hand in hand with customer service. In fact, I think of quality as preemptive customer service.

## JUST LIKE THE PRINCESS AND THE PEA

Mother's Day '97 was the busiest in the history of our company. One of our floral designers complained about Ike, the store manager in Manhattan. We had done over 1,100 packages that day. As the designer described it, "We were totally crazy busy, barely keeping up, and all of a sudden I see Ike coming off the back of a truck. He has a package in his hand, already beautifully and elaborately wrapped. Ike brought it back to me to redo because he thought that one of the lilies was too transparent and wouldn't hold up for very long. I think this is nuts, especially on our busiest day of the year."

When I heard that story through the company grapevine, I called up Ike and personally thanked him, because he is letting it be known that we are sticklers for quality, even on our busiest days. That's a message I want our employees to get, and it is definitely a message I want out there with our customers. We use technology to increase our orders and efficiency. We hire people who feel a relationship with and a responsibility to our customers. We care about quality. Any customer who doesn't respond to those aspects of our organization isn't from this planet.

## Chapter Nine

# Press # to Talk to a Real Person

An alarming thing happened on the internet on January 1, 1996. 1-800-FLOWERS was named the single most successful business application on the World Wide Web. I say "alarming" because after all the hype about the way the internet is transforming our lives, to have our little company come in ahead of Microsoft and IBM tells you something about how far the web has to go before it begins remotely to fulfill the predictions we see in the television commercials.

In those commercials, wanting and doing are the same thing. Want to design a school in India without leaving your desk in New York? Want to identify an ore sample while it's still wet on the riverbank in the Brazilian rain forest? Want to know who's playing at the jazz festival in Puerto Vallarta?

Want to find a new mate? Get rid of an old one? Read the latest letters to *Penthouse*? Raise capital? Unload a company?

The answer in the commercials is "The web will make it happen." It's as easy as point and click.

Maybe someday, but not yet. What I want to know is "How is it going to happen? And when?" I think that is what we all want to know. But we are just at the beginning of all this. Predicting the growth of the web is like trying to predict the earthquake that will one day rock California. We all know the Big One is coming, but how big? When? And where? Only the event itself will provide that answer.

## THE MARTHA STEWART FANTASY

We Americans have always prided ourselves on being self-reliant, or, even better, self-sufficient. We have this fantasy that if we managed our lives correctly we could do everything from home and have completely fulfilling lives. Martha Stewart in her little corner of Connecticut, all by her lonesome, can grow a garden, refinish her floors, prepare saffron lobster risotto for twenty guests, and crochet her drapes out of old prom dresses and Christmas ribbons. The fantasy is, if we were all as accomplished as Martha, we could live a perfect and tasteful lifestyle all on our own, never leaving our supremely tasteful cottages.

To extend the fantasy, with the aid of a computer and a modem, the modern worker has no need to leave that perfect home to go and earn a living because we can all tele-commute, handling personal interchange through E-mail or the headset we plug into our phone and wear all day.

Finally, in order to acquire the necessities of modern life—from fresh produce to the hot new CD *Yanni at Niagara Falls*—all we have to do is dial up the internet and ask our Alta Vista search engine for "organic baby jicama," or "drippy+New Age Music+on location+waterfall." The desired web page comes up. You give your safely encrypted credit card number and you're done shopping.

At this rate nobody will ever have to talk to anybody face-to-face and we can all sit in our underwear in front of computers all day typing away, ordering goods and services without ever leaving home.

B.S.!!!!!

It's a nice fantasy but it's not going to happen. Sure, some people will use the new technology to become at-home professionals, but working at home isn't for every-body. Distractions known as spouses and children have a way of barging in at any time of day or night to ask where the hairbrush is, or can they borrow your car to go to the movies, or how do you solve a quadratic equation? I believe that most people need to work in a social environment: they need the contact around the watercooler. They need the competition, the high fives when they succeed, the sense of common purpose. I wouldn't know how to manage a corpo-rate culture of stay-at-homes. Much as we may cherish the fantasy of working at home, we basically need to get out of the house. In short, no matter how good computers get or how cheap cell phones become, the workplace will not disappear.

Similarly, neither will the mall. As you see every time you visit one, a lot more than shopping goes on there. Shopping, in addition to acquiring goods, fulfills social needs. We go shopping because it's fun. It's a social experience, whether it's one-on-one bargaining, looking to see what stylish people are wearing, or just hanging out with friends. Like the traditional workplace, traditional shopping provides contact, and contact is a fundamental need that is not met in the stay-at-home workplace or through internet shopping.

Look at a current internet success story, Amazon.com. If you know what you want and that's all you want, it works. But there's more to it. If Amazon.com is the be-all and end-all of book shopping, how come Barnes & Noble, with its easy chairs and Starbucks Coffee bars, is doing so well? Because when people go shopping for books, the book is only one part of the equation in the shopping experience. The stimulus, relaxation, excitement, and the encounter with the new and unexpected are the reward for the book shopper who leaves home. Browsing is fun; your web browser isn't.

In short, technology in general and information technology in particular are altering the workplace and the way we buy things, but more by way of supplementing traditional shopping. Computers offer convenience, but sometimes it's social contact that we crave much more. Those companies that learn to exploit computers and information technology to connect socially or to entertain will, in my opinion, reap the greatest benefits.

## IT TAKES TWO TO INTERACT

Take out your magic markers and underline this, please: *The web isn't interactive—people are.* A computer is not in and of itself an interactive tool. For that matter, neither is a telephone. For true interactivity you need a person at either end. This is the great secret to building an internet business. Simply putting up a catalogue on-line and then waiting for net surfers to tap in their credit card numbers is a waste of a web site. There's nothing involving about it, nothing to draw customers in, to make them feel confident and welcome, inform them, or entertain them. If you don't do all of the above, someone else will. That someone will reap the business rewards.

A great military thinker once said, "War is the extension of politics by other means." By the same logic, the internet is the extension of commerce by other means. It must fulfill the same functions of any other retail system. 1-800-FLOWERS has been in on-line commerce for more than six years. It was a natural jump for us from telemarketing to modem marketing, so when CompuServe and America Online came along, we got involved. It was pretty much a no-brainer.

The first thing we learned is that, as with any other retailing operation, you need infrastructure. You need a way to keep track of inventory, process orders, secure billing, and deliver product. Take it from me, none of this is automatic. There are bugs, glitches, and snafus galore to work out just as there are in any new marketing venture. Fast or slow, however, there are still start-up costs and a different learning curve for every business that sets up shop on the web.

Right now, 10 percent of our business is on-line. This is significant, but much more important than new business are the new customers who have begun to shop at our web site. Although it may surprise those of you who think of flower-giving as a basically female activity, roughly half of our customers are men. But on the internet, 75 percent of our customers are men, and follow-up research tells us that many of these men are first-time flower buyers (probably apologizing for having ignored wives, moms, and girlfriends while they sit zombified in front of their computer terminals).

We've seen an even bigger bump on the international side. While international orders represent less than 5 percent of our business, 10 percent of our on-line business comes from overseas, much of it from Americans who recognize our brand, trust it, and can now send flowers back home for the price of a local call (as opposed to the larcenous rates that most foreign phone companies charge even for an 800 call to the United States).

So, yes, there is great promise on the internet and, yes, consumers are demanding that merchants offer this new access channel, but, just as true and of paramount importance, they will only come back if they are satisfied. And customer satisfaction is and always will be a one-on-one proposition.

# THE COMFORT FACTOR

Those of you who have placed orders on-line may recall the first time you were asked for your credit card number. You felt a little hesitation. Would someone steal the number? Would your order reach the right party? Would the company follow through or would you disappear down some black hole on the web? We have had hundreds of savvy computer types place an internet order and then call our toll-free number to make sure we got it. This is the digital equivalent of wearing a belt and suspenders.

This taught us a valuable lesson: internet merchants must nurture customer confidence and not leave it to blind faith in new technologies. We must market smarter and use the new tools to learn more about our customers and how to satisfy them. Godiva, the up-market chocolate maker, provides a perfect example of how to use interactivity to better service its customer base. When customers visit their web site to place an on-line order, they are offered a 10 percent discount if they answer three questions about their preferences. The next time the same customer orders, he or she is offered another 10 percent discount for answering three more questions. What could have been a simple transaction now becomes a powerful tool in building a customer database.

# HEY, WHAT ABOUT NUMBER CRUNCHING?

Although I never tire of pointing out the interpersonal potential of new technology, I don't mean to suggest that computers are simply cyber pet rocks best used to make us all feel warm and cuddly. What I am saying is this: beyond brute hardware and software, the great opportunities in digital commerce await those who discover the most involving social interface.

At the same time, I would like to restate the obvious: computers compute. With or without the internet, they are great number crunchers. If you know how to ask the right questions, they continue to provide business advantages to creative thinkers. It all goes back to my belief that if you can measure things, you can improve them. Wal-Mart is a tremendous example and one that I turn to whenever I feel we aren't using all those spare gigabytes that my information services people tell me I absolutely have to have to survive.

Last Christmas season there was a toy that Wal-Mart predicted would be its best-seller. So far, no great shakes. We all make sales projections, but Wal-Mart threw some very sophisticated random access technology and parallel processing at their predictive model and they were able to make this projection on very little raw, in-the-field data. By August, they had placed the item for a test in two stores, one in California and one in Michigan. They sold seventeen items, and on the basis of that microscopic sample they doubled the size of their order!

Normally, I would say that Wal-Mart was playing retail hara-kiri, but the proof is in the way it played out. They knew from having hired the best brains and thrown the most sophisticated equipment at it that they could have confidence in their model. If things didn't respond according to the model, they would tinker with product placement in the store, with lighting, and, only as a last resort, with price. They didn't like this last option because discounting means your model is wrong.

This kind of predictive modeling—which told them precisely how much sales they could project given X amount of promotion—is something that no amount of human resources could have accomplished. It needed computer technology. Come December 22, three days before Christmas, they were able to meet their projection and sell out. Now that's what I call a well-planned Christmas season.

There are three things I learned from this event:

*First*, keep looking for new ways to measure. The more you measure, the more information you will have. The more information you have, the better able you are to take action with confidence.

*Second*, if you just use your computers for database management and simple bookkeeping, you are giving away a competitive advantage. Go for the highest use of your technological infrastructure and not simply a way to automate all the rote stuff.

*Third*, if you have to compete against Wal-Mart, find another business.

## YOU ARE HERE (WHERE THE HELL AM I?)

I think of technology as a continuum and the present as a point on that continuum. It's like those maps of the shopping mall, with the arrow that says, "You are here."

"Here" is the present. The growth of information technology is the rest of the map. It includes not only those things that are presently up and running but the ones that will be built: not only the level that you are on, but the levels above and below you and the additional levels that will be added on five years down the road.

"What good does that do me right now?" you might ask. I cannot give you a more complete answer than to tell you that I know that something is going to happen and you have to be around, be in the game, if you expect to benefit from the changes and growth that are going to come. And though I cannot predict exactly where we are going, I know that technology is going to play a large part in determining where and how fast we go.

## B~~ANK~~S INFORMATION IS WHERE THE MONEY IS

Consider this fact: If you took the family fortunes of the Rockefellers, the Vanderbilts, the Fairchilds, and the Morgans and *doubled* them, you would still not arrive at the net worth of Bill Gates. The fact of the matter is that today's information age industrialists have far surpassed the fortunes created in the days of steel mills, oil wells, and manufacturing. Information technology is where the new fortunes are being made.

The challenge for us who are building our businesses today is to figure out where we are in the continuum of the evolution of technology because no matter how good your company is doing this year, in order to do better next year it will have to do more with less—i.e., increase productivity—and the only way that is possible is to reengineer the workplace by deploying efficient new technologies.

So where does all that put you? There are no sure bets, but there are some likely scenarios based on what we have all seen happening over the last few years:

- Hardware is going to get cheaper.
- Memory is going to get cheaper.
- Applications are going to get more compartmentalized.
- Optical disk storage, which will represent an enormous leap in our ability to store information, will become a reality.
- Networks will become a bigger factor.

## HELP! I NEED A RAM IMPLANT!

Do you know what you get when you put an infinite number of workers at an infinite number of computers? They give you the same output that you get from that infinite number of monkeys that type everything from Shakespeare and the Bible to Zxwzklllfrmpnogg. We need ways to organize and *edit* information before we drown in the trivial and the ridiculous.

As information technology takes over more and more of the economy, successful businesses will be those who use technology to do new things. Using new tools to do old jobs will not get you very far ahead of the pack. Word processing allowed all of us to write more reports more efficiently. The result? Instead of the paperless office, we are drowning in paper. E-mail is a great communications tool, but it also is the greatest thing ever invented for covering your butt by allowing you to cc: the world. There is a flood of information out there. Too much for anybody to comprehend. Infinite information is no more going to make you a more successful entrepreneur than an infinite amount of salt will make a better chicken soup. The trick is not necessarily to get more information. It is to use information technology in ways that will free up your human resources for more productive use of their time.

Which gets me to my business and how we deploy technology.

There is nothing particularly high-tech about giving somebody a gift of flowers. It isn't even low-tech. No-tech is more like it. Yet somehow I have become the Internet Posterchild. Both AT&T and Apple have plastered my face all over nationwide advertising campaigns. Why me? I've been looking at the same average guy in the mirror for enough years to know that it isn't my Mel Gibson–like looks that got me those jobs.

It was technology. Technology is the buzzword of our age.

I believe in technology. I built my business on technology, information technology. I use technology everyplace that I can. *But I mistrust it too.*

## TIME—THE CURRENCY
## OF THE NINETIES

Whenever anyone comes to me and touts the latest whiz-bang interactive gotta-have-it piece of software or hardware, I am reminded of what Robbie Robertson, the great guitarist and songwriter from The Band, used to say when people came to him with new showbiz ideas: "All right, but does it pass the Who Cares Test?"

Think about it: What are the possible reasons to deploy a new technology?

- Your competitor uses it.
- You want to have more gigabytes than anybody in the business.
- It got a great review in *Wired.*
- It will speed up the handling of some of your operations (even if there is no crying need for speeding them up).
- You have an old version of the same program.
- Your nephew, the one who solved *Myst* in a weekend, thinks it's cool.
- It will give you more time to spend with customers.

To my mind, time is the big issue here because when all is said and done, technology does something with the laws of physics that escaped Einstein: it *creates time*. Time is a key advantage in a world of increasingly intense competition where it is less and less possible to get, and hold, an edge in product. The business that can use technology to create time by shrinking the inefficiencies in its systems will hold on to its competitive edge. That is what Wal-Mart did in its Christmas model.

Time is so valuable that one thing our people hear me say over and over again is, "Time is the currency of the nineties." Because I believe that time is that important. By saving time, shrinking the inefficiencies, our company has averaged 50 percent growth through the nineties—and we have not raised prices once in more than nine years! No matter how you slice it, this is a tremendous competitive advantage.

Think about it. I sell a lot of flowers, but I am not going to improve on the rose. It's just not going to happen. God did a fine design job and he isn't really looking for any partners. But, through technology, I can process your order more quickly, confirm your delivery more accurately, and remind you of birthdays and anniversaries more faithfully than my competitors.

How do I do this?

Technology helps, but it also helps a lot of other businesses in handling this kind of repetitive noncreative work, whether it's reading the price of a box of Froot Loops at the checkout counter or giving you instant approval for a car loan. But we use technology to do one other thing. We turn to technology to free 1-800-FLOWERS employees to devote themselves to the kind of human contact that I had with

Norman when we planted tomatoes. In other words, we use technology to create time to create relationships to create customers. The sales are the benefit that always follows.

## COMPUTERS AREN'T FRIENDLY, PEOPLE ARE

The point of all this is that technology isn't enough; it must have a goal. Nine times out of ten my goal is creating the opportunity to build relationships. Mining time sounds great, but in the retail business it is simply not enough. Just as with any mine, a time mine yields high-grade and low-grade ore. The mother lode for the successful time miner is that much-mentioned but never-used concept: quality time. Any way that you can free up your people to interact and form an emotional bond with a customer, as Dave the milkman did at my grandmother's, is so valuable that I cannot even begin to quantify it. It's the whole shooting match.

## LOVE AND WAR AND A PINK CORSAGE

I have a hit list that I go down whenever one of my people proposes a new piece of technology—or any innovation for that matter. First question: How will it improve our value proposition for our customers? And if it does, how will they notice it? Value created without value perceived isn't going to do us a whole lot of good.

Which gets me to the real heart of the matter: How will it improve our word-of-mouth advertising? If it doesn't, then I am probably not interested. But if it does, customers will perceive greater service on our part, greater satisfaction on their part. They will come back as repeat customers and they will talk about their experience with their friends and relations. This kind of business is the equivalent of a prospector finding a nugget of gold lying on the ground. It is "free business." You see, we need four or five transactions to pay for the new customer that we acquire by advertising or marketing. With word of mouth, we can be profitable from gardenia number one.

Take a recent Valentine's Day. We got a call from a World War II vet. Like millions of other kids in the forties, he went off to war with the memory of a pretty girl in his hometown. But four years of war change a lot of things, and when the young soldier came back from the war, he had his sights set on a life outside his little New Hampshire village.

Time went by. The soldier married and raised a family. Then as youth turned to old age, he lost his wife. He called us because he had never forgotten that young girl from the innocent days before he went to war. "Could you find her?" he asked. Our supervisor heard about this call and knew this was the kind of challenge that I just love our company to take on. With encouragement from her, the rep hopped on the case. One phone call led to another, and finally we found a recently widowed woman in the same small town who seemed to fit the bill.

The old soldier sent her a corsage that was a duplicate of the one that he had given that girl he never forgot the night of the prom, when they danced real slow to "Moonlight

Serenade." The card said, "If you're the Mary Anne that I left in '41, I'd sure like to get caught up with you."

She was. He did. 1-800-FLOWERS got the order for their wedding flowers, a great item in a lot of small-town newspapers, and you can bet that we also got a whole lot of referrals because one associate took the extra time to do something thoughtful. It was the oldest kind of human connection, but it was new technology that got us into the databases, allowed the supervisor to get involved, allowed the rep to switch her calls to another station, and so on.

## CUSTOMER TIME IS GOLDEN TIME

Technology allows us to redeploy our human resources to maximize the relationship-building aspects of a transaction. As we just saw, we have a very sophisticated monitoring system that allows us to assess how well we are doing on our calls and, just as important, how we can improve. One thing we are not interested in is how long a call takes. Where most businesses want to know how quickly you can take an order and get off the phone, we are interested in how well you service the customer. We know that is going to take a little longer, but it is the only way to build a relationship with the customer. There are many other ways in which all the millions of dollars we have spent on software will save us time. But when one of our people is in that almost sacred realm of personal transaction with the customer, we want to get the most out of the opportunity.

## 86 ZILLION MEGABYTES — SO WHAT?

I think many people of my generation are impressed with the features of new technology before they ask themselves, "Are they needed?" As the father of a few Generation X children, I can say that I think they have a much healthier attitude toward technology. If you come in with a new gizmo I am the kind of person who is usually wowed by it. My natural techno lust takes over. Gen Xers are much more pragmatic. They want to see the functionality of the thing. They want to know how and in what ways it will do things differently or better. While you or I might stand there with our hands in our pockets marveling at the coolness of a new piece of tech, my kids' generation grew up around technology, so if it doesn't do something practical, their attitude is "Next, please!"

While it's true, as many have pointed out, that technology can depersonalize business, my unshakable belief is that the most successful entrepreneur will be the one who figures out how to inject personal contact into the new relationships that grow out of technology. When I say personal contact, I mean real contact with a real person. Nothing annoys me more than dialing a number and getting sentenced to ten minutes of button pushing while some actor with an overly friendly voice leads me through a dozen layers of menu-driven choices. And by the way, if they really need all those choices, why can't one of the first ones be "If you need to speak with a real person, press #"?

This is not personal contact. This is more like the creepily friendly loudspeaker loop in *Bladerunner* recruiting unsuspecting rubes for the frozen gulags of "the Off-World." Real personal contact involves an interactive relationship. If you are the customer, you are more likely to feel fulfilled and come back again if you sense that there is a real person—at the other end of the phone, at the other end of the web—who can respond to you and care.

If you can accomplish this through the use of technology, then you will build customers in the old-fashioned sense of having a relationship with buyers who are *accustomed* to dealing with you because they feel more secure than they would in dealing with some anonymous seller. On-line, on the phone, across the counter—it doesn't matter how you make contact. It's the contact that's important.

People want contact. The closer it is to face-to-face, the better. Using technology to create new opportunities for human interaction is our guiding principle. In the 1980s, 800 technology enabled us to offer a new level of personal involvement with each customer. At the same time, information technology was growing more and more powerful. Now, the second our phone rings, our telereps already have your credit card info, your purchasing history, likes, dislikes—a whole profile. Instead of wasting time recapturing old information, the rep is freed up to talk, probe, get more deeply into servicing the customer. This is a good use of technology because it injects more of the human element.

# NO TECHNO-ZOMBIE
# VAMPIRES, PLEASE

At the other end of the spectrum, we came across another piece of technology that allowed us to pick up the phone before the caller even heard a ring! We thought this was pretty cool. Callers hated it. They thought it was downright creepy, like we knew what they were doing before they did. They expected a normal call where the phone was picked up after two or three rings, so even though we had the technological means to do away with phone rings, we chose to stay with the old-fashioned ring cycle because people felt comfortable with it.

The story doesn't end there. That same technology allowed us to adjust the length of the phone ring. Before this technology, at superbusy times like Christmas, we had the not very great choices of putting people on hold with canned music or letting the phone ring more. But we already knew that people like to be picked up by the third ring so we simply extended each ring from six seconds to nine seconds. We found that there was no perception of a longer wait. So with the same number of rings, we were able to serve people better during the holiday rush without turning them off with too many rings or too much "elevator music." Their first contact with our company happened when a real, live person answered their call—a big plus.

## CONFESSIONS OF AN ON-LINE SUPERSTAR

Make a relationship, then do business. It's the simplest piece of advice I can give you, but the most valuable. The relationship is the transaction. The exchange of money and goods are just the external sign. Technology can extend your reach, multiply your contacts, but you still have to make contact.

At a conference a few months ago, my brother Chris, who is our senior veep of operations, was seated next to the top software development person for a major on-line service. I can't tell you the name of the service, but their initials are AOL. When she mentioned that she was a regular customer of 1-800-FLOWERS, Chris asked her if she ordered on-line.

"Actually, I order by phone," she answered, with a tinge of embarrassment.

"Huh?" said Chris. "You work at this major on-line service and you place your personal order by phone?"

"Hey, I spend the whole day looking at a computer. I want some human contact."

I rest my case.

## Chapter Ten

# Entrepreneur, 46, Needs Job

You know you have reached a plateau of success when you look at your skill set and then look at your employees and you realize that there is someone better at every one of your skills. In my case, I have better flower arrangers, more efficient telereps, better long-range financial planners, more intuitive human resources people, faster telephone installers, more web-savvy internet experts.

This is a good thing. It is also a crossroads. Some entrepreneurs have no problem with this turn of events, but others never seem to be able to get through it.

Get over it! You can't do everything, and the more you try the worse you will do. I speak from experience.

As 1-800-FLOWERS began to grow, there was more and more work to do. I decided that the solution was to simply sleep less. Using Tony Wainwright, a savvy ad agency CEO, as my role model, I tried to get by on four hours of sleep a night. For a few months, I actually thought I was succeeding.

Then Mother's Day rolled around, and I am guessing that I hadn't slept more than six hours total in the previous four days. I had a meeting in Dallas and took a late plane the night before. I was so exhausted that I passed out in my seat. The crew couldn't wake me up. They said I was in a semi-coma, and they were about to call the ambulance. I came to and convinced the crew that I was all right, or at least all right enough to make my way off the plane and over to my hotel room at one in the morning. I was due at a big meeting at 8 A.M. With a lot of effort, I dragged my butt to the meeting, but I felt like hell. My skin was taut, I had the sweats, and I was mentally out of it.

Shortly after this near-death experience, I saw the light. I was invited to give a talk to an IBM audience at the Kennedy Center. Dr. Jim Maas, the well-known expert on sleep, was also on the bill. He had written a book focusing on the importance of sleep in obtaining peak performance. It wasn't long before he had convinced me that there is a reason that most people get about seven hours of sleep a night—we need them! This, for me, was the ultimate "wake-up call."

My company, your company, any company, doesn't require someone who can do everything all the time. Why have an organization if that's the case? Unfortunately, many of us have enough middle-class guilt that we still feel we have to be there all the time. But there are plenty of people in our company other than me who are perfectly capable of taking an order at two in the morning. If I have an early meeting with a prospective marketing director or the president of a bulk-mailing operation, I will be worth more to my company and my employees if I am sharp and on my game. In much the same way that I recommend using technology at its highest level, I think you have to look at key executive talent (and I regard the boss and founder as pretty key) the same way. "Highest use" is as true for people as it is for technology. (I can say this and in fact believe it, but I have yet to completely accomplish this.)

## PERFECTION IS STUPID

Your job description changes when seen in this new light. You are no longer the engine of production, the foreman, the head of sales and personnel. You are the manager of a process. This requires a change of outlook and a redefinition of standards.

I recently walked into one of our stores. Right off the bat I saw some things that I would have done differently. I could have made a simple suggestion like "Hey, why don't you reuse the garbage pail liner? If it isn't dirty or wet, why use a new one?" Sure, we might have saved a few cents on Hefty Bags, but I would have interfered in the process of the business. And make no mistake about it, every suggestion from the boss has a tremendous ripple effect.

Embracing process means having faith in your people

and letting them do their jobs. Yes, you will suffer inefficiencies. But a big company that is 90 percent efficient is going to make a hell of a lot more money than a one-man show that is 100 percent efficient. A larger enterprise is by nature fraught with a certain level of inefficiency. Your job, then, is not to achieve perfection but to reduce inefficiency to a M.A.L.O.S.U. (Maximum Acceptable Level of Screw-Ups).

It is my belief that you do this by creating a culture where people can do their best work. They will do this if they enjoy their work, i.e., if it is, in some sense, fun. They will do this if you foster a culture where they feel connected to each other, to the company, and to you. Connectedness optimizes the flow of energy, ideas, and effort within the closed system of the company. The more unobstructed the flow, the less tension, and the greater the chance to achieve economies of intellectual and emotional scale.

## WHERE DO IDEAS COME FROM?

When I talk about optimizing connectedness and creating an easy flow of energy, I am not talking about flat hierarchies or offices without walls. In some cases those cultural styles work, and in others they decidedly wouldn't (for instance, the Pentagon). I simply mean that the more ways you can find to connect your people—and fun is the best way I know of—the more easily ideas will be presented and get a full hearing. This is so important as your company grows because inevitably the entrepreneur who started the whole thing begins to become insulated from everything except the ideas and style of his or her inner circle. The day becomes one long meeting with little room for spontaneity and virtually no contact with the front lines.

This may make you feel important, but it cuts you off from the energy that made you a success in the first place. You need to be in touch with all levels of your company and especially with the people who are dealing with your customers. That is why I take every opportunity to mix and mingle with our people in all kinds of activities: flipping burgers for summer barbecue lunches or taking a few people to a conference who might not ordinarily be invited.

Recently I hired Susan for a senior management position. She holds an MBA from NYU and had been a rising star at American Express where she ran customer reward programs. I like the culture at American Express. It is a brand that I recognize, and it stands for certain values and ways of doing things that would be good for our company. AmEx differentiates itself by its respectful service relationship with customers. They don't play with your name on mailing lists, send junk mail, and the like. AmEx says, "Membership has its rewards," but I get the feeling that another part of their credo (and certainly the basis of ours) is, "Your customership is our privilege."

I knew that Susan felt a natural nervousness about leaving a major worldwide company in order to come to the middle of Long Island to work for an entrepreneurial organization— a florist. I wanted to get over that right away so I invited

Susan to join me and my communications director on a trip to visit some of our BloomNet florists even before she began work.

It was good for her to get out in the field and meet our florists, and, equally good, we all got to hang out together, have dinner, and do business in a social context. This served a serious business purpose, because when Susan showed up at our home offices after the trip, she already knew the company. Additionally, she and I had fast-forwarded our relationship. She had seen the boss outside the office structure. Just as important, I now knew how she thought, spoke, laughed, etc. I could read her shorthand, so to speak, and she could read mine. Our working relationship could now get off to a much quicker start. We understood each other.

Of course you can't do this with every new hire, although as much as I can I usually take a few people with me on those trips. I always try to find some way to get together with people informally whenever I am on the road. It could be as simple as showing up at one of our call centers in the morning with a bag of donuts and a dozen cups of coffee. I round up a group according to no special plan, and we sit around and talk about family, football, the weather, even business. It opens up some lines of communication that inevitably pay off down the road. I may not always get a new money-making idea from an interchange like this, but I get a sense of our people and they get a sense of me, and the next time I see them in the break room it becomes that much easier for them to approach the boss and make a suggestion.

# THE NO-CALORIE LAYER CAKE — THE BIRTHDAY FLOWER CAKE

One of our best money-making ideas came from a bull session on one of my trips. We had visited a number of our BloomNet florists. BloomNet is a nationwide network of 2,500 flower shops that we have handpicked to fulfill our orders. They have the right customer service attitude and take service seriously. As we talked with florists in a number of towns, I kept hearing the same message: "We want to be able to do something more with our craft capability." It made sense, come to think of it: if you are in the flower business, the odds are you have an artistic bent. You want to do something more than wrap up a dozen roses and send them out with the driver.

One night, toward the tail end of the trip, I brought up this subject with a group of florists. It just so happened that Lily Buckland, one of our fulfilling florists near Denver, was celebrating her birthday. That night we all went to dinner at one of those Rocky Mountain places where they serve you a steak the size of a German shepherd. We fell deep into conversation about what we might do by way of a new offering for birthdays—something that only a florist could do. At that very moment, the lights dimmed and the waiters filed over with a big beautiful birthday cake with sugar flowers all over it. As Lily took a deep breath to blow out the candles, a little light went off in each diner's well-fed brain: "A-ha! What about a birthday cake made entirely of flowers?"

The next day, before we flew out, I went down to one of our BloomNet shops and a bunch of us clipped stems and wove leaves around a wire frame and made a prototype birthday flower cake. Good idea, but the cake wasn't there yet.

We sent out the word to all of the BloomNet florists. Could they submit a design for a birthday flower cake? The winner would get a trip to New York with their significant other and two tickets to see Whoopi Goldberg in A Funny Thing Happened on the Way to the Forum. One of our Long Island florists, Carolyn Ahmad, worked with my sister Julie and with key associate Jerry Rosalia. Together they dreamed up an incredible cake design. We went with it. The Birthday Flower Cake is the single most successful design we have ever had. If I hadn't taken the time to hang out and go to a dinner with some of our people, we would never have done it.

It pays to keep every line of communication open because one of these days, right out of the blue, a valuable message is going to come down it.

## EVEN A GREAT IDEA ISN'T ENOUGH

People tend to think of entrepreneurs as people who build better mousetraps: they invent things. It could be the Polaroid camera, or Club Med vacations, or personal computers.

In the popular mind, the entrepreneur is someone who comes up with a new idea, believes in that idea, and makes a lot of money from that idea. The key part that is left out in the popular mind is the organization that takes the idea and makes money with it. So in addition to raising capital and selling a vision, the entrepreneur creates a culture. He or she may not think of it as creating a culture, but whenever you bring people together in the workplace and organize them for a common purpose, you are creating a culture. Everything you do contributes to the way that culture will run. Will it run by fear or through persuasion, hierarchically or in total anarchy? Either explicitly or implicitly, you make these choices, and they come to characterize your organization.

I prefer to enter situations with my eyes open and to understand how my behavior affects my enterprise. When you realize that your actions have consequences that shape the nature of your organization, you can begin to have a plan.

## CREATING WINNERS

My job at St. John's was almost pure cultural engineering: trying to affect the behavior of a group in a predictable and positive way. The background these kids came from was, in effect, structureless. Life had no plan; it was simply a question of surviving the crisis of the day. Your objective was not to get killed in gang violence, not to be abused by adults, not to starve. Structure, plans, group effort, mutual reenforcement—none of these things were part of the picture. We wanted to introduce all of those elements into the life of each of our boys, but it was like trying to teach them a new language.

The earlier we got to them, the better chance they had of succeeding. Additionally, and just as important, if they came in understanding some of what we expected, they would be less disruptive with the rest of the boys.

Early on, I hit upon the idea of the entrance interview. I would make the kids sit through a series of interviews before they came to stay with us. What I knew—and they didn't—was that they had already been accepted. I gave them the impression that they had to pass through these interviews before we would take them in.

Right at the get-go, then, the boys had the feeling that you had to be special to get in. Through word of mouth it got around that we didn't just take any old underprivileged street punk. We had "standards." When you know that a place is tough to get into—whether it's a private school, a posh restaurant, or, as in our case, a halfway house from street life—everything seems a little bit better when you finally do get in.

I would probe deeply at their first interview. Were they having a problem in school? With drugs? With parents? Gangs? I tried to get all the difficult stuff out in the open from the start. My favorite question, one that I still ask in almost every interview, consistently got revealing answers. Somewhere toward the end I would ask, "What am I going to see in your behavior a year from now that you wish you had told me today?"

For some reason that question hits a hot button. Everybody tries to put the best face on things at a first interview, and everybody has something that they hold back. When you acknowledge this by asking this question, it's like saying, "Hey, you know and I know that a lot of this talk is what you think I want to hear. How about giving me the lowdown?"

It was like giving someone a license to tell the truth. The stories would come pouring out. Oscar told me how his mother was a hooker—a piece of information about Mom that your average person would probably not volunteer at a first meeting. I learned that Raheen had taken part in a gang beating that had nearly killed two kids from a rival school (and that he would have been beaten if he hadn't). There were little brothers who hated big sisters and little brothers who loved them; kids who had been selling drugs since third grade; kids who had never had a Thanksgiving dinner; kids who had never had a ride in a new car. Everyone had a different story to tell, and everyone told me one detail that made them stand out as a person and gave them individuality. People go into an interview trying not to call unpleasant attention to themselves, but if you ask the right question, every person has something they really want you to know, a fact that will make them rise in your estimation or, just as often, a fact that will cause them to be cut some slack down the road.

At the end of the first interview I would open my appointment book and set up a second interview. I invited several senior staff people to sit in on this one. Again, the boy thought it was all part of the process to gain admission, when, in fact, it was a way of beginning to get them used to the program as well as a first introduction to many of the key people with whom they would be interacting after they came to the home.

Then, after the boys had cleared this supposed hurdle, they were asked to come to spend a day at the group home, the culmination of that being an interview with the house-mother, which in the context of all this interviewing and supposed evaluation made her into quite a big deal.

It was very instructive to see the effect that this whole process had on the boys. Simply by having to go through a structured program and having to pass certain levels of inter-viewing, they began to sit differently, behave differently. They were proud to be there, even excited. They had finally achieved something that the straight grown-up world recog-nized! Even better, they had succeeded at something, per-haps for the first time in their lives. The side effect of this whole process was in reality the main reason that I instituted it: I was able to introduce the boys to our whole culture at the group home without their ever knowing it.

## PLEASE DON'T CALL YOUR TEACHER #!@%&*

Every boy who came to the group home could invent curses that boggle the imagination. If these kids had been paid by the word, and you took the most common Anglo-Saxon oath out of their vocabulary, they all would have taken a 50 per-cent pay cut. There are all kinds of sociological reasons that explain why cursing is such an important part of the culture: rage, social impotence, creating emotional space, etc. But I wasn't particularly interested in the reasons for this behavior: I knew that cursing was the kind of "lower-class behavior" that would keep them out of the job market, or at least the decent job market. And if these kids couldn't get decent jobs, then they would end up in jobs where cursing didn't hurt their career advancement: hit men, enforcers, drug runners, soldiers in gangs.

I started a cursing fund. Every time one of the boys let fly with one of the generally recognized four-letter words, he was fined 25 cents. The money went into a kitty. Up to this point, the strategy was not much more enlightened than washing mouths out with soap. But now for the part that made it work. These kids liked cool clothes, probably because most of them didn't have many. A kid with flashy threads got noticed on the street even more than the kid with the foulest mouth.

Using my old connection at Dadson's, I talked Ebb Weissman into giving us a discount on clothing we bought for the group home. Ebb had his soft side too.

When the kitty reached a certain level (with some secret help from the pockets of the staff), the kids who had managed to cut out cursing went down to Dadson's and picked out some flashy shirts. The foul-mouthed boys got nothing.

During the time when Bill and Ernie were trying to enforce school attendance so that I would take them on the camping trip, it was truly funny to watch them try to cow the other boys into toeing the line. Without profanity, the boys were tongue-tied! But somehow they managed to get their point across. I wouldn't say that the daily level of discourse ever reached a point of common civility, but still it was nothing my grandmother couldn't have listened to. On second thought, make that my daughter; Grandma heard her fair share of blue language in the contracting business.

The point of this cursing fund was to take us toward a goal. To help these boys along, I needed to create a different kind of culture within the home, to make it a transition to the real-world workplace. I found a fun way to modify behavior and created incentives to bring that goal about. Twenty years later, I have changed jobs, but I still try to do the same thing.

## IT'S NOT WRITTEN IN STONE

Every company is a unique organism. What works in one doesn't necessarily work in another. The company you were five years ago may be entirely different from the company you manage today: same name, same product, but totally transformed. Your job as cultural engineer is to be so connected to your people that you understand how their needs change along with the company.

For instance, at 1-800-FLOWERS, we have been through at least three dress codes. Dress code number one, in the early days, was Come As You Are. We were basically a bunch of working-class people from Queens, and we tended to dress in jeans or khakis for the men, skirts for the women. There weren't a whole lot of coats and ties. That was fine as long as we were running our fourteen-store operation out of a basement in Bayside. I mean, how much more impressed would someone have been if I had worn a coat and tie, given that my "office" was in a walk-in refrigerator?

When we bought 1-800-FLOWERS, the whole nature and scale of our business changed. We needed many new telereps and supervisory personnel. For the first time, we were a "real" company. I wanted to attract people who were looking to begin a serious career. In some way we had to meet people's expectations of what a bona fide important company should feel like.

If I was going to get the best out of them, I had to show some respect for their workplace. We bought a few truckloads of Herman Miller office furniture—top-of-the-line stuff, nice-looking, comfortable and, therefore, pretty expensive. Many of our employees looked at the job as a step up in the workplace, the first rung on the ladder toward career advancement and fulfilling the American dream. Jeans and shorts were out. We went to shirts and ties. The attitude of professionalism in the air was palpable.

Now, ten years later, we began to feel strong resistance to ties and dresses. Casual is in. Everybody wants to look like the guys in the Dockers commercials. But if we said, "Wear what you want," we would be back to jeans, and I know that would take the professionalism down a peg.

Chris and I were stumped. We didn't want to look like Mary Poppins at the bank office with all those starch-collared old fogies. But I didn't want to look like the extras in a Metallica or Bone Thugs 'N Harmony video either. We asked Vinnie McVeigh to convene a few roundtables, and the idea that came out then was shirt and tie or 1-800-FLOWERS logo wear. We have long-sleeved polo shirts with our logo for the winter and short-sleeved for the summer. No major gripes so far (and I have acute gripe antennae).

Our case was totally different from Microsoft, for example. We had many kids from a lower socioeconomic background, and it was important that we treat the workplace as something special and a step up. Structure and a certain degree of formality meant we were treating them with respect. Microsoft employs a lot of young people from middle- and upper-middle socioeconomic backgrounds. They had been through the shirt and tie thing and watched their moms and dads go to work in "business attire." To attract the kind of people they wanted, it was important for Microsoft to be informal: Birkenstocks and PIBs (Persons In Black).

One of the greatest cultural engineers I know is Jerre Stead. Chris and I really like him a lot and have managed to spend a fair amount of time with him so we could steal his ideas. Let me put that another way: We wanted to pay tribute to his farsightedness by instituting some of his groundbreaking innovations in our own company.

Bob Allen hired Jerre to work at AT&T, and shortly thereafter, when the company acquired NCR, Jerre was given the job of integrating the two cultures. NCR was a white shirt and dark suit kind of place. It looked like an office in a 1950s documentary about conformity. When I went to visit Jerre at NCR, I saw a lot of these formerly stiff-looking execs in khakis and golf shirts. Jerre's message was "things are going to be different" under the new regime, and he chose the dress code as a way of making a statement.

Then, a few years after that, Jerre went to work at Ingram Micro in California, the capital of laid-back casualness. Guess what? Jerre went to a shirt and tie look. Once again he wanted to communicate the fact that change was in the air.

## WHAT YOU DON'T HEAR CAN'T UPSET YOU

The workplace breeds pressure, rivalries, and animosities. For the most part people are there because they need the paycheck, not because they have an inborn love of the job. Nor do most people like taking orders, especially when the person giving them is under the same kinds of pressures and sometimes is gruff or heavy-handed. In this kind of environment, to use a current sporting term, people talk a lot of trash.

Ignore it. That's easy to say, but it took me a long time to learn. I remember one day on the job with my dad. It was hot. The job was in a lousy neighborhood and we were way overbudget. Walls turned out to need replastering, and there were old leaks and water stains under the accumulated coats of paint that had been put on carelessly for the last forty years. My dad, fearing that we were going to have to eat the added expense because we had misestimated, was very short-tempered.

The mood was infectious. After laying into two of the workmen for sloppy work, he left. There I was on the scaffold as these two guys cursed my father out something fierce. I leapt to my father's defense and quickly became embroiled with my coworkers.

When I told my dad what had happened, the only reason he didn't clout me for good measure was that I looked so bedraggled. "Schmuck," he said by way of consolation. "You're the boss's son. Of course they're going to curse me out. You have to ignore it. Now I have to fire those two idiots and where do you suppose I am going to get replacements for that miserable job? I know they don't like the job and they don't like me, but the important thing is they were doing their jobs!"

This was true insight from my father. Selective hearing is an important skill for any boss or manager to develop. People are always going to blow off steam in the pressure cooker of the work environment. If you allow steam to dissipate, it will cool and become harmless.

Another person who taught me about selective hearing was Joan Dalton, one of the wisest people at the St. John's Home.

Joan was a strong Irish lady, married to a New York City cop and the mother of eleven kids (she gave birth to nine of them at home!). When Joan came to work for me as a secretary, I saw that here was a woman with deep personal resources: warm, organized, smart. Though I hated to lose her as a secretary, I saw in her a major talent who could serve the organization at a higher level than as my assistant. So, within a year, I put Joan in charge of some of our support services, which entailed maintenance, housekeeping, food services, and purchasing. These were tough, grisly guys she had to deal with, New York City workmen with a big attitude. I very clearly remember needing to talk with Joan one day when we were both under a lot of deadline pressure.

"I have a million fires to put out today, Jim," she said. "If we can talk on the run, fine."

Joan wasn't kidding about the crises. We were up for a review by a state agency. Added to that, Christmas was coming on, which always made us scramble to make something special for the boys. From plumber to electrician to deliveryman, Joan, while not exactly on the warpath, was all business. Everyplace Joan went, the carpenters complained about the plumbers, the plumbers complained about the painters, food services complained about the supermarket. Everybody complained about the higher-ups in the organization (which included Joan, me, and Brother Tom). And, thrown in for good measure, they all cursed a blue streak as soon as our backs were turned.

"How do you deal with these guys?" I asked. "It's infuriating."

"Selective nonhearing," Joan explained. "I am only interested in important issues. That's what you pay me for. Side comments aren't part of my job description. Plus, I really don't want to hear what they are saying about me, or you, or the place in general. What good will it do me? We'll just have more fights and less will get done. I hear what I need to hear and ignore the rest."

I have found this to be among the one or two sagest pieces of advice that anyone has ever given me on office dynamics: Hear on a have-to-know basis. The rest is just static.

## Chapter Eleven

# The Brand Called "You"

In life, you have a permanent record. It's called your résumé. These days, it is the rare employee who spends a whole career with one company. Companies that we all thought would be around forever are cutting back, going out of business, changing their businesses. Companies that we thought were the wave of tomorrow, like Apple Computers, now appear to have been no more durable, with no more of a lock on the future than Bob the blacksmith was a hundred years ago or Ronnie the record player repair guy was in my childhood (have any of your kids already asked, "Daddy, what's a record player?"). The only career constant is change, change so fast it can give you whiplash. We seem to have been teleported to a parallel universe where the old rules of employment physics no longer hold.

# WHAT'S A DOWNSIZED GUY SUPPOSED TO DO?

I used to see Marty at the country club. I never really knew him very well. He was just a familiar face. He was an upper-level guy at Grumman, which was a big-time employer in my part of Long Island in the days of mega aerospace contracts. From World War II until the end of the Cold War, son followed father and grandson followed them both, working for Grumman, filling the gazillion-dollar orders that we all thought would last forever.

The only problem for Marty was that "forever" happened one day in 1993. The Cold War ended, the contracts dried up, and Marty's "peace dividend" was a pink slip. Fifty-two years old, a lifestyle based on a salary of more than $100,000, benefits up the wazoo, and out of a job. Marty approached me one day after a round of golf and asked if we could talk for a few minutes. He wanted some advice. I said sure and ordered us a couple of beers.

We talked about the possibilities out there for Marty. We even touched on his coming to work for us, but he knew and I knew that his skill set was in just one industry; worse, it was in just one company. He may have been worth a hundred and a quarter at Grumman. But at 1-800-FLOWERS we didn't make jet fighters or guided missiles. Managing the inertial guidance system for the F-14 didn't have a whole lot to do with the price of gardenias in Chile, or how many wedding anniversaries are coming up in Ohio, or how many deliveries we project for National Secretary's Week in Taos.

"I'm just going to have to sit tight and wait for the right thing to come along. I can't afford to go to work for less than a hundred," Marty said, believing that he still held a few good cards in his hand.

Maybe he was right about what he could afford. But six months later, six months of knocking on doors in competition with a lot of other downsized guys, and Marty was back. Not at the club this time. I didn't see Marty around the club as much. Those greens fees start to add up when there is no paycheck coming in.

Marty wasn't so concerned with what he could "afford" anymore. He no longer needed a hundred thou before he could even consider a job. He didn't need $75,000. He needed a job. Hell, he could probably squeeze by on $40,000. "It sucks big time out there," Marty confessed, telling me what I already knew. "My kids have better jobs than I do. I need something, anything, just to get out of the house."

I've taken a few shots on guys like Marty over the years. I don't anymore, even though it kills me to see someone in his position. But here's what happens. I hire him because, hey, it could have been me. And he comes to work for me with the best of intentions. But the first job that comes along that pays ten grand more than I do, he has to take it. It has nothing to do with loyalty, gratitude, or what kind of a person Marty is. It is basic survival.

The solution for Marty was not so much in finding a good job after he was downsized. The real solution, the thing I tell every employee, and which I never stop telling my kids, is "Never stop learning, never stop your education, and most important, never stop doing things on the side." In other words, never stop "résumé-ing" (and yes, I know I'm using it as a verb).

## HASN'T MANNY SANGUILLEN BEEN PLAYING FOR THE PIRATES FOR SEVENTY-FIVE YEARS?

If you understand this basic principle, then what you have to do to succeed—make that survive—is not to put your faith in one company or one skill. You need to build a résumé that embraces lots of skills. It's like those utility infielders in baseball. They aren't the big home-run hitters or the fireball pitchers, but somehow those guys who are good with a glove, who can play a few positions, who can lay down a bunt—in other words, who have a varied skill set—those guys always seem to have jobs. If one team outgrows the need for them, another will pick them up.

So if you can't control the long-term future of your company, then it is no longer a question of "putting in your time and staying out of trouble." The only thing you or I can really control is "What do I do with the time that is available to me?"

Second jobs are a good way to prepare for your next move. In fact, the flower business was my second job, one of many that I had over the years. It wasn't always a question of taking the first decent job that came along. I constantly asked myself something much more important for the long-term game plan: How does this job match up against the Three Requirements of Second Jobdom?

## The Three Requirements of Second Jobdom

### 1. What is the income potential?

Although we all work for money, this is not always the first concern for the second job. Sure, we could all use the dough but more important . . .

### 2. What is the potential for self-improvement?

The change agent in today's culture is based not on gold, inherited wealth, social position, or physical strength: it is based on silicon and those little microchips and how well you interface with them. Ask yourself, "How will your side job improve those skills?" It may not, in which case you are going to have to pick them up somewhere because, barring the second coming of the Great Flood or an invasion of space aliens, the only thing you can absolutely count on is that technology will drive more, not less, of the future economy. And if aliens do take over, they will probably value technological skill even more than Bill Gates (who, come to think of it, just might be a technologically savvy alien himself).

Of course, you might already be the most computerized person around, but if you don't have social and professional contacts, you are just a dweeb sitting in front of a screen. No matter what you do in a second job, you need to learn how to make contacts, and that is why you must also ask yourself . . .

### 3. How will this job improve my people skills?

When I was just starting out, looking for a second job to keep me going, I could have made reasonably good money as a carpenter's assistant, but that wasn't going to stimulate me mentally and it wasn't going to widen my circle of contacts. On the other hand, working as a bartender, a job for which I felt my Irish heritage had genetically programmed me, helped me break down my natural shyness and taught me how to interact with people. Less money but more contacts.

# THE HOLLYWOOD METHOD (OR, HOW BIG IS YOUR ROLODEX?)

The paradigm for the company of the future isn't General Motors. It probably isn't even Microsoft. Giant companies with enormous payrolls just don't make sense anymore. Instead of making a company secure, bigness just makes for a fat target. There is one industry, however, that seems to thrive in good times and bad; one that I have never heard anyone refer to as a good place to look for long-term business lessons. In fact, just the opposite. It's a business that most of us think is no more than a big crapshoot and run by the biggest flakes in the world. I'm talking about Hollywood.

In the future, I believe businesses are going to look more and more like a feature film production. Did you ever look through all the credits at the end of a movie? There are hundreds and hundreds of people there. Carpenters, drivers, dialogue coaches, lighting experts, directors, assistant directors, associate directors, assistant associates, and on and on. As many people work on a feature film as in many small companies. But the difference is, a film crew—from star right on down to the kid who gets the donuts—is a bunch of freelancers possessing a variety of skills who come together for a single project.

As for the actual company or business? There is none. In the beginning a film is just a person with a telephone and a Rolodex: the producer. In business terms he or she is an entrepreneur, somebody with an idea and the ability to sell that idea. When the idea is sold, the producer starts making the phone calls to assemble the skills needed to make a film. No different, really, from a contractor building a house. How does the producer know whom to call? He or she goes on track record, which is another way of saying résumé. A résumé begins to answer three questions:

1. What is your skill set?
2. Who have you worked for?
3. What will other employers say about you?

In other words, what can you do, for whom have you done it, and what will they say about you? You are the one who has to learn the skills, use those skills in a recognized company in the marketplace, and earn high marks for your skills and for yourself as a person. Hourly worker, middle-manager, senior VP—the requirements are the same. Since companies and jobs no longer last forever (forget about forever—sometimes they don't last as long as your career), everybody, including you, is an entrepreneur. You are building your own business with one product for sale—*your skills*—and one brand—*you.*

Well, if I, as an employer, can't offer you a lifetime career, what can I bring to the party to make you want to put in the time at 1-800-FLOWERS rather than WIDGETS Я US?

I can help you build your brand.

## THE NEW EMPLOYER CONTRACT: THE COMPANY BRAND RUBS OFF ON YOUR BRAND

I just hired three senior management professionals, highly skilled and, because of that, highly paid. One came from McDonald's, another from Citibank, another from IBM. I liked them. I was impressed by their skill sets. I knew and liked the cultures they came from. What I owe to them and to everyone who works for me is to make 1-800-FLOWERS into a culture and a brand that will mean something to them as they go forward in their careers. How do I do that? By following the following:

# Three Rules for Employers in the Twenty-first Century

### 1. Keep Your Brand High in the Sky

The days of lifetime employment with a single company are over. While we tell all our staff that we hope they will be with us forever, the reality is that only a few of them will.

For the majority, "musical jobs" will be the norm rather than the exception. When they are ready for their next job at another company, they will have higher perceived value if they come from a company with a great reputation. People who have worked at a "hot brand" company—Microsoft and Starbucks are two easy examples—will command more in the open market. As an employer, my responsibility is to manage the brand of our company and to ensure that it remains as high as possible.

### 2. Run a Well-Managed Company

A well-managed company will likely be one with a great brand reputation. But there are other aspects of a well-managed company that are the responsibility of employers. Compensation programs, health benefits, and a stimulating work environment are a few of the hallmarks of this kind of high-quality company.

*3. Invest in Your People*

Today's employers have a responsibility to provide their staff with challenging, creative work. To prepare for serial employment, the associates must be conscientiously "résumé-ing"—pursuing skills that will enhance their employability.

Floraversity, our in-house and industry training program that now includes an on-line version, is one of the commitments we've made to our staff. Another is the regular rotation of job assignments, which keeps team members fresh and constantly adds to their skill sets.

# THE NIKE OF THE NET

A few years ago we outgrew our telemarketing facility. Actually, using the word "facility" makes our setup sound a whole lot grander than it was. How about a bunch of crates and boards and telephones down in the basement of our Bayside, Queens, store? Within a few years of moving north from Texas we outgrew Bayside and moved to Westbury, Long Island. And then, as the idea caught on and it actually looked like my multimillion-dollar crapshoot wasn't going to land us in a group home for busted entrepreneurs, we moved to our present locations and acquired the capability to handle millions of calls a week.

That transformation started with four words.

"We need a bridge," I said to Sharon Cain, a young woman who had joined us as a telerep and whose gung ho participation in our company softball and volleyball teams marked her as a dogged competitor. If the world is divided into people with lots of flash and people who can crank it out, no matter what requires cranking, then Sharon is a champion cranker-outer. Whatever task you throw at her, she dives into it, sponges up the information, and organizes things. The Sharon Cains of this world are like the master sergeant who runs the motor pool in the army. They know where everything is and how to get anything done, even if it means a little rule bending.

"A bridge?" Sharon said quizzically, not knowing for the life of her why our business would need a heavy piece of civil engineering.

"Not a Brooklyn Bridge–type bridge, but a bridge like on a ship or the starship *Enterprise*. You know, a command center where you can monitor activity, give directives, manage the flow."

That's all I had to tell Sharon. Not knowing any more about how to build a telecommunications bridge than a toll bridge, Sharon jumped in and found out what she needed to know about state-of-the-art, high-tech equipment. She set up a system that worked for us for years.

With that task accomplished, I threw another job at Sharon and another and another. Then, about six years ago, I start to sense this tingle, just like the tingle I got that day when I was shaving and I first heard about 1-800-FLOWERS and thought it was such a world-beating idea. Tingle #2 was the internet. I didn't really understand exactly how it would build our business, but I did know that it was the technological wave of the future and that technology was the horse I had bet the ranch on and would continue to back.

If I were to feel that tingle today, I would be able to hire a high-priced expert. But back in 1991, there were no experts on internet commerce. There were futurists (a futurist is someone who you pay a lot to tell you what is going to happen and then you sit back and wait a couple of years before you find out that you wasted your money). Call it my Irish blarney detector, but I didn't see any reason to get a clueless person from outside to start our internet business when I had plenty of clueless but capable people inside our company who had never let me down in the past.

By this time, Sharon had handled about eighteen (I am not exaggerating) different jobs for us. So I unleashed her on the internet. We are a company that has always done a lot of phone business, and the internet uses phone lines. I began to notice how the AT&T people, the Apple computer techies, and the CompuServe marketer all developed that glazed "I give up look" whenever they visited Sharon. They would emerge from the telemarketing center goggle-eyed, with their pocket protectors frayed from whipping out their pens to answer Sharon's questions. At that point, when they looked informationally drained, Sharon would reduce them to quivering jelly when, instead of saying, "Thanks and good-bye," she would invariably pipe up with "Just two more questions, please."

Bottom line, six years later Sharon is an expert on the internet. She went to school on the job while a whole new industry was conceived, birthed, and brought to ripe adolescence. We teamed her with Donna Iucolano, the incredibly talented woman who heads our interactive services division. When the rest of the world was wondering which way the wind was going to blow, Sharon and Donna set our sails and brought us to that brief moment in time when we were the number one retailer on the net.

Sharon is what I would call a Nike woman. When everybody else says, "How am I going to make this happen?" Sharon, Vinnie McVeigh, Joan Waters, and two dozen more of our core people answer, "Just do it."

By relying on our own internal resources, we gave Sharon Cain the chance to lap the quantum physicists at Microsoft in terms of actually wringing some dollars out of the internet. As a company, we showed our present and prospective employees that 1-800-FLOWERS is a place where you can grow.

## THE REEBOK ROTATION:
## CAREER CROSS-TRAINING

Our growth has always exceeded our skill sets. Just as I learned to be a telemarketer because the other choice was to go financially belly up, we have, time and again, had to ask our people to try new things. And just like Sharon, they usually rose to the challenge. Not without a few screw-ups, mind you, but I believe there are no advances if you don't take chances.

The upside is more confident people learning to do more things, increasing their value to our company as well as the value of their résumé. In the beginning, we didn't have many skilled hands so we learned by doing, and as we did we began to see the virtue that grew out of the necessity to use the best available, if slightly underqualified, hands.

Now, twice a year—once in the spring and once in the fall—Chris goes around the company and asks a few dozen of our most promising people, "What size shoe do you wear?"

Chris, I assure you, does not have a shoe fetish. He returns with two dozen sneakers and hands them out: it's "moving day," and we begin a little career cross-training that we call the Reebok Rotation. Loren, from accounting, moves to customer service; Josephine goes from the telecenter to accounting. Further up the executive food chain, Tom is no longer a controller, but a retail operations manager.

The idea is that people get to try different jobs, acquire different skills, make new relationships (or redefine old ones), and absorb more of our culture. True, the mistake level goes up but sometimes a fresh outlook, a new way of looking at things, leads to opening up unsuspected new possibilities.

I have to confess that the Reebok Rotation was an idea I never would have had if it hadn't been forced on us by our breakneck growth. Now that the company is a little more mature and we have brought on some highly paid and highly specialized role players, it gets a little harder to play career musical chairs, but it is a great thing for any young company to try and even older companies should at least make the effort to keep circulating personnel.

## THREE GOOD REASONS TO MOVE PEOPLE AROUND

1. It builds everybody's skill set, making them more valuable on the job market.
2. It reveals hidden talents and new approaches that invigorate the company.
3. It establishes a culture by which your company's people are known as they move into the wider job market.

## MAKE THAT FOUR REASONS

4. Of course, as in everything else we do in business, moving people around into new roles is another way of creating contact and making connections. Until people are connected, their interaction is limited. Much is made of teamwork as a corporate metaphor, but I sometimes wonder if executives are so fond of talking about it because of its rarity. It's kind of like men in prison talking about women: it is because they don't have any that they are obsessed. Teams grow naturally if people want to play together.

## Chapter Twelve

# The Art of Making Mistakes

Shortly after I opened my first flower shop in Manhattan, I found myself neck-deep in roses as Memorial Day approached. This is not where you want your neck on that particular weekend. For a florist, the next worst thing to no business is too many flowers. You can't mark down your inventory and recoup your costs with a sale. The roses wilt and you are out of pocket.

Not a good way to go into my first summer in the business. When you have zero cushion—and you should have known better than to dig yourself into that hole—it will put the fear of God into you and your business.

So there I was contemplating how I was going to tell Marylou that our plans for Memorial Day weekend were going to have to downsize a little bit—there being a direct connection between how many flowers we sold and how many steaks and cases of beer we could afford for the family barbecue. Then, late one afternoon, the phone rang. It was the wife of the Cuban ambassador to the United Nations. She had been invited to a party at the Kissingers' and wanted to bring something spectacular. By the way, don't be too surprised that Henry Kissinger was fraternizing with Cubans. There's a reason they call them diplomats: They know how to get along with one another.

Mrs. Ambassador had a vision of what the perfect party gift would be. She said, "I know it's really late on a holiday weekend and you're probably completely out of roses, but I keep seeing three double vases filled with huge bouquets of long-stem roses."

"Mrs. Ambassador," I answered, "whatever it takes, I give you my word I won't rest until I find those roses for you." By 7:30 we were at the apartment with the vases, which looked quite dramatic on the piano and the breakfront. It must have been $400 worth of gorgeous roses.

We were sold out of roses. I went home that Saturday night with a smile on my face and a hunger for the first charcoal broiled T-bone of the summer.

# WHO'S PERFECT?

Show me a businessperson who says he or she doesn't make mistakes and I will show you a liar. Everybody makes them. If you don't make them, you are not taking risks. Capitalism, contrary to what you may have learned in Economics 101, is not simply about understanding the law of supply and demand in the marketplace. Capitalism is about taking risks. Taking a risk means sometimes you misstep, but missteps don't mean you are a failure. Even a big boo-boo doesn't make you a worthless schlemiel. Crying and drowning in self-pity, trying to fix blame, staying angry: these things will hurt you much more than a bad hire, a bad investment, even an ill-conceived product.

# J. P. MORGAN'S BIG MISTAKE

The next time you want to kick yourself for having missed an opportunity, remember you are not alone. History is full of the stories of great men who missed the boat. The important thing is they eventually caught it. I often think of the story of Thomas Edison and J. P. Morgan. Morgan was one of the shrewdest, maybe even *the* shrewdest businessman who ever lived. When Thomas Edison invented the electric lightbulb, he went to visit Morgan in the hopes of raising $200,000 to become partners with him in wiring and lighting Manhattan. Morgan, so the story goes, thought it was a harebrained idea and gruffly showed Edison the door.

Edison, totally on his own dime, worked for the next two years to wire a half-mile square of Manhattan, which just so happened, very uncoincidentally, to be the half mile surrounding J. P. Morgan's house.

When Edison finished the wiring, he returned to Morgan's house, placed a lamp on Morgan's desk, and turned the light on. When Morgan saw that he could actually read easily at eight at night, he promptly wrote Edison a check for $3.8 million. I can just imagine the old billionaire huffing into his big silver mustaches as he wrote out the check to Edison.

What can we learn from this?

- First, it's nice to be able to write a $3.8 million check to correct an oversight.
- Second, it's nice to see that even big shots make mistakes.
- Third, the best thing to do with any mistake is to realize you've made it and move on from there. In other words, do something positive. You cannot undo the past; you can just do better next time.

## BAD NEWS, BOSS— EVERYTHING'S GREAT

One of the companies on whose board I serve has a credit manager who very proudly reported a decrease in bad debts to less than one-tenth of one percent. He positively beamed as he delivered these incredible figures. You have never seen a man look hangdog more quickly than that credit manager when the CEO jumped all over him.

"What can be better than zero bad debts?" the aggrieved creditmeister wailed.

"You aren't taking any risks. You are not being liberal enough in looking for new business opportunities. Lowest possible and lowest optimal receivables are two different items entirely."

I think this is true in anything. If your daughter scores 100 on every math test, it's time to get her into a tougher class. If your son wins every track meet, he should be competing against better runners. In real life no one bats a thousand. So in business, as in everything else, I mistrust a perfect record. If you don't lose sometimes, you are not going up against the big-time players. You are leaving business around for someone else to pick up.

Competition is often described as the unquenchable desire to win. Yeah, that's part of it. But just as important is the lack of fear of screwing up and making mistakes.

Recently our business came full circle, and we have begun to expand back into franchises. In the same way that 800 telemarketing had to become multichannel and embrace the internet, we also realized that the on-premises retail business was a vital and overlooked area in our business model. It has been years since I, or any of my associates, have been involved in the day-to-day ins and outs of a franchise operation.

I knew going in that we would make mistakes, lots and lots of mistakes. That's okay. I told everybody at the outset, "We are in this for the long run. If we only hit the 10th percentile in our plan this year, I know we will learn, and next year we will be at 40 or 50 and then 60 or 70. We may not get it right the first time; that is almost a certainty. But we will stay with it until we get it right."

I accept mistakes. To a certain degree, I welcome them as the sign of a company that is trying new things. The only thing that I really ask of myself and the people I deal with is, "Try not to make the same mistake twice." If you do, then you have every reason to get down on yourself, and you can be reasonably sure I am going to be on your case too.

# GET OVER IT!

If you are interviewed by Barbara Walters, I suppose you have to expect to be asked, "If you were a tree, what kind of tree would you be?" That's part of the Barbara Walters drill. Likewise when a business magazine comes to interview, one of the questions that is supposed to make you feel like getting real candid with the interviewer is, "What is the biggest mistake you ever made?"

The last time someone asked me that, I thought for a few seconds and then, half ironically but with more truth than not, said, "I think I just made it."

"How do you mean?" the reporter asked, somewhat at a loss.

"Spending time thinking about my biggest mistake is a mistake. The key for me, both personally and professionally, is to recover quickly!"

Mistakes have a way of sticking around like guests who come for dinner and who are still telling jokes at two A.M. while you are trying to gently coax them out, having changed into your jammies and yawned publicly, loudly, and often.

Soon after we bought 1-800-FLOWERS, Chris told me about a great deal just waiting for us to snap it up. A supply company was going out of business, and we could pick up the contents of their warehouse for a song. So we rented the trucks and carted out endless quantities of file cabinets and other bulky items. We stored the goods in the basements of every one of our stores. What a steal! We were going to be sitting pretty when we needed all this neat office stuff.

Guess what? For the most part we needed those office supplies the way a fish needs shoes. Five years later, we were still throwing heaps of it away. File cabinets, carbon paper, three-hole punches, i.e., lots of stuff that we had less call for in the digital age. I shudder to think about the storage bills we incurred because the basements of our stores were filled with discount office supplies instead of flowers.

"Too many good deals like this," I said to Chris, "and we're out of business."

## PEOPLE MISTAKES ARE THE TOUGHEST

Splitting up partnerships and firing people are two of the hardest things in business. The mistake we all make is procrastinating. We all see ourselves as nice people, and firing or breaking up are not nice things, so we put them off. This is not doing anyone any favors. It's bad for you and bad for the other person.

Jack Welch, the CEO of General Electric, who is, in my mind, the paradigm CEO, hit the nail on the head one day when we were at a reception at our local hospital. He asked, "When was the last time you said to yourself, 'Gee, I wish I had waited six more months to fire that bastard'? It never happens. Always err on the side of speed. You will never make a mistake."

By waiting too long to fire a guy, I nearly lost a piece of my leg. It happened out at the St. John's Home. We had a guy on the maintenance crew who wasn't maintaining. I don't know if he was drinking, or if he was just plain not very good at his job, but whatever the reason, it wasn't working out. I knew it. He knew it. Both of us stewed on it. I think he reached the boiling point first because one afternoon I came into work and my assistant, Jane Geraghty, said, "Uh—Jim— I'd be careful if I were you. Larry is in there and he has his German shepherd."

While I had no qualms about firing Larry, and had known for a while this was coming, I really hadn't planned on firing his dog too. And how do you fire a German shepherd? "Uh, listen, Rinny, this is tough for me, but things haven't worked out like we hoped. It's not you. God knows you're one helluva dog. I think it's just you have too nice a bark to be a fearsome watchdog. Did you ever look into Seeing Eye work?"

Somehow I didn't think that was going to work with Larry's shepherd, who, by the way, wasn't Rinny. I think his name was something more like Horst.

I walked into my office and there was Larry holding Horst on a chain. Horst bared his teeth and growled. I had prepared myself by picking up a big metal stapler from Jane's desk.

"Larry," I said, "I don't have anything personal against you or your dog. But if you don't take Horst with you and leave this office and don't come back, I am going to kill your dog. I may have to kill you too, but I am certainly going to kill him before he tries to kill me. So I am going to count to ten, very quietly, to myself. And if you are still here and the dog is still here, then the dog dies."

Threatening Larry wasn't going to get me anywhere. Threatening his dog put the fear of God into him. Larry walked out of my office and I never saw him again. It never should have gone that far. Norman Mailer is reported to have said, "Relationships that don't get better, get worse!" He was talking about romances, but that's doubly true for on-the-job relationships.

## FRIENDSHIP IS TRICKY

I have often heard it said that you don't do business with friends. Easy to say; not so easy to do. Entrepreneurs, people like myself, who don't draw clear lines between work and family and friends, inevitably end up doing business with friends. You can't help it, or at least I can't. For the most part, I revel in it. Still, with the greater sense of trust and openness that comes from dealing with friends, there is also a risk to the friendship if things don't work out. This is not an original thought, but for some reason we all think we are the ones who are going to show that we can rise above this old caution about doing business with friends. Forget it. It never happens. Your friendship is always on the line when you do business with an amigo.

Friendship is an equality relationship. Business isn't. If you are both on the same team in business, one will be the boss and one will take orders. One will inevitably do better than the other. The spontaneity, the frankness, the ease of communication, that are the basis of a friendship are the first things to go when it becomes a business relationship that doesn't work out the way you'd hoped.

I thought my friendship with a guy I will call Jerry (because that is not his name) was strong enough and I was a sensitive enough guy that we could venture successfully where other friendships have cracked up.

Jerry was from my neighborhood. We went to grammar school together. His dad drove a delivery truck for a cake company. When Jerry and his wife, Doris, got married, Jerry's dad got him a job with the conglomerate that owned the baking company, and the newlyweds moved up to Rochester, New York. But Jerry and Doris were dyed-in-the-wool New Yorkers, and after a few years among the folks that we "sophisticated" city types used to call "apple knockers" (because upstate New York was where all the apple trees were), they moved back down closer to home, settling in New Jersey.

Jerry did all right with the cake company, but it's always somewhat of a struggle when you work for a salary. You get by, but somehow you keep falling further into debt. Meanwhile my little flower business was growing nicely. We had four or five stores at the time, all turning a profit, but it was never enough to finance our expansion outright. I always had to borrow, mortgage, or beg to come up with the cash for the next store.

All through this time, Jerry and I were best buddies, and he would often mention to me that he wanted to do something on his own and could he throw in with me? I said sure, not realizing then what I have since painfully learned: There is no such thing as a tag-along entrepreneur.

I borrowed some money from the credit unions and took another $25,000 mortgage on my house, and Jerry did the same. And just about then, another friend gave me a tip on Washington Public Power Systems bonds (later known as WPPS—pronounced WOOPS—bonds). Since I didn't need the cash that very moment, I figured I would park it for a short while in a safe investment.

Six months later, WPPS goes belly up and I am out $25,000. Believe me, that hurt a lot. But instead of pissing and moaning, which would have done me no good at all, I went in hock for more and we opened the store with Jerry in charge. We did pretty well at the outset. Then Jerry started not to be there a lot: he had family problems. But the flower business is one business where you need to be there to run it. Actually, I suppose that's true of any business, but I speak from hard experience in the flower business.

Our business wasn't getting Jerry's attention, and it began to flounder. Doris blamed me for somehow taking Jerry in and pulling a fast one (never mind that I had lost my initial investment and was mortgaged beyond belief). "I told you so," she said, which was the first time I had heard of her opposition.

Neither Jerry nor the store was performing. I fretted and stalled and finally went to Jerry and said, "Look, this isn't working. You're miserable. I'm not happy. Your wife is starting to hate me. I don't want to lose your friendship over this. I'll buy you out. I don't have the cash, but I can pay you back over the next three years."

Those were the right words, but he knew and I knew that our friendship had taken a body blow. He accepted my offer.

But Doris, who completely mistrusted me by now, was sure I was up to something. When the store finally became profitable a couple of years later, it was "I told you so" all over again. According to Doris I was wrong to involve Jerry in the first place and wrong to buy him out in the second place.

She was right . . . in hindsight. No matter how well that store did, and it did very well, it was just a store. There are always a thousand stores out there waiting to open, but in life you make few best friends. Be very careful before you mix your business and your best friend, because, as Jerry and I learned, there can be consequences.

## AND THEN THERE ARE GOOD MISTAKES

You may not believe it but I am a shy guy at heart. At one time I was very shy. It is something I had to work very hard at to overcome. For the most part, I am well over it. However, when I had to shoot my first commercial, I was like a seven-year-old kid again, the night before the school play: "God, maybe you could give me a heart attack so I don't have to wear that frog suit in Sister Denise's class?!"

My prayers went unanswered back then, so I knew better than to waste God's time asking him to bail me out of this commercial. The director was an ex–New York Knick named Luther Rackley, an extremely funny and easygoing guy. The shot that he had set up had me in front of a display of flowers. It was all laboriously lit (there is no such thing as an easy lighting setup when you are doing commercials). The only problem was, Luther is very tall, much taller than I am.

He must have set the lighting for an NBA player because when I stepped into the shot, all you saw behind me was a vase—no flowers. I was too short. Given the lighting, it was easier to change my height than to rearrange the flowers. The only way they could get me and the flowers in the shot, then, was from a low angle, shooting up. So they put a towel on the floor and I did the commercial on my knees. I felt so ridiculous that it really loosened me up, and the finished spot had a very loose and friendly feel that I have since tried to capture in every commercial that we do. That was one mistake that worked in my favor. If everything had gone according to clockwork, I would have frozen up tight.

As a footnote to that story, I can't resist getting in a dig at one of our oldest employees (in length of service). Jerry Rosalia is an excellent florist who has been working for us for so long that you needn't even ask me what he does. Let's just say that he is our spiritual leader. He was an extra in the commercial with me—one of a number of people walking around in the background, working at the cash register. For some reason, Jerry kept stopping the filming to get his makeup fixed.

Finally I blurted out, "Jerry, for God's sake, you're just standing there in the background, what are you constantly running to makeup for?" Don't get me wrong—Jerry is a sweetheart and the soul of our company, but he is never going to be mistaken for Tom Cruise, and no amount of makeup is going to put him in the heartthrob category.

"Sorry, Jim, I won't be a second," Jerry would say before going to have his nose powdered.

After an hour of this, I needed a quick touchup on my makeup and I saw why Jerry had to constantly have his few remaining hairs futzed with. The makeup artist for the extras was the most amazing-looking woman in five counties. She was built to kill and dressed in jogging wear that did nothing to conceal her amazingness.

"Jerry, you're fired," I jokingly said as I returned for my closeup.

## Chapter Thirteen

# Confessions of a Shy Guy

As I said, I was a very shy kid. People find this hard to believe now that I have the public persona of a guy known for talking to groups, cracking jokes, walking up to people and introducing myself. Once upon a time, however, the first day in a new school or with a new team I was a mental case. And girls? I might as well have been from a country where English wasn't spoken.

I beat my shyness the same way I beat my fear of flying years before. I took a deep breath and ran straight at my fear.

## FEARLESS FLYING

I wasn't always afraid of flying. As a kid I loved it—all dressed up in a white shirt and checkered tie because I was going on an airplane! It's funny how far we've come and how blasé we get about things that used to be a major big deal. Anyway, when I turned eleven, I was called upon to chaperone my grandmother when she went to visit her family in Providence, Rhode Island. Why would an eleven-year-old boy have to chaperone Grandma (my mother's mother, not the one who worked in the construction business)? Because Grandma wasn't too wild about flying, and once we were airborne she'd throw back three Manhattans. As far as Grandma was concerned, she probably felt she was perfectly capable of flying without a plane.

I had fun on those trips anyway. I liked planes. No problem. But phobias are a funny thing. As soon as our first baby, Erin, was born, I developed tremendous anxiety about flying. I was sure every time the pilot came on the loudspeaker it would be to deliver tragic news:

> "Ladies and gentlemen . . . crackle, crackle . . . this is the captain speaking . . . uhhh . . . crackle, crackle . . . apparently two of our engines were improperly bolted on, and they have fallen off. We expect to crash in approximately ten seconds . . . uhhh . . . but we'll have a nice view of Hartford as we descend."

Each time I took a plane I could only envision worst-case scenarios. I would insist on the exit row. Then I started to obsess that some lackadaisical ground-crew guy had probably left the exit door ajar and that I would be sucked out at thirty-seven thousand feet.

John Madden is enough of a big shot that he can insist on a bus and the rest of the world is happy to work with him on his own schedule. But as a fledgling entrepreneur, I couldn't expect anyone to cut me any slack. If I was going to make it in this world, I needed to get on airplanes and go after business, meet suppliers, attend conventions. Drinking myself into oblivion wasn't an option. I find that a heavily hungover person does not make a great first impression at business functions. I would have to learn to fly right through my rough emotional weather.

At that time Marylou and I were part owners of a ski house up in the Catskills. Nearby there was a fellow who flew in air shows: dips and rolls and other aerobatic stunts. I think his showbiz name was Rick the Rocket.

I screwed up my courage one morning and walked over to Rick's hangar, which was in a barn by a cornfield that fronted on a grass airstrip.

"Ricky," I said, "what do you charge for a ride?"

"Well, to cruise over the falls and have a look at the mountains, we could make it twenty bucks because you're a neighbor. It'll cover the gas."

"How about if we stay up a little longer, I give you fifty bucks, and you do your best to scare the hell out of me?"

I got my money's worth. Ricky did power dives, stall-outs, loop-de-loops, figure eights. We buzzed the local farmers and then flew so low over a pasture that I could have patted the heads of the cows. Or, more accurately, I could have patted the animals if my eyes weren't closed tight as I prayed fervently for deliverance from this madman and his airplane. Ricky did everything he could to make me lose my lunch, and I obliged. But, and this is the important part, I began to overcome my fear of flying.

## BECOMING AN EX-SHY GUY

Getting a job at Dadson's haberdashery (what a great, old-fashioned term!), in addition to getting me out of the painting business, was, as flying would be later, a frontal assault on my fears. To sell clothes, you had to connect, and even if I wasn't a glad-hander, I had to learn to play the part. I learned to say—and sound as if I believed—things like:

> *"You know, you're lucky, you have the kind of shape that they design for. You can wear it right out of the store without any alterations."*

or

> *"A lot of people couldn't get away with wearing a purple sport coat. You really make it work."*

These are the kinds of things you need to say, and say convincingly, if you are going to succeed. I wanted to succeed, so I learned how to gab. It was at that same time in my life that I discovered that humor is the great icebreaker. It is the single aspect of social interchange that makes people feel comfortable most quickly. Even if the joke stinks, you have extended yourself, made an effort to reach the other person on a basic human level. The contact works even when the comedy doesn't.

One of the things that interested me about the work at St. John's was that it required developing new social skills. Talking a gang armed with knives and chains (in the days when it was still rare for inner-city teenagers to carry guns) into putting away their "toys" and leaving the home in peace was not a job for the tongue-tied. You had to threaten, sweet talk, cajole . . . and *survive*.

## THE C.E.O. AS HOST

One of the best ways to overcome shyness is to assume the role of host. If you are busy trying to make people feel comfortable in a social situation; if you keep working the room, making sure that people who don't know each other are introduced; and if you start conversations and then work your way out of them so that they can proceed without your participation, then you are so consumed with your social agenda that you forget about your shyness.

My secretary, Patty, is (or was) very shy. I began to give her hosting responsibilities at various gatherings that I had to organize. There were lots of VIPs to handle: business heavy-weights, politicians, celebrities. Patty did just fine. After one of these shindigs I complimented Patty on her work and she replied, "Thanks, but I still don't think I could ever get up in front of strangers and give a talk like you did."

"But Patty," I countered, "what did you think you were doing when you went around the room and made sure that everyone was taken care of and introduced?"

"Oh, that was different," she said. "I was working."

"Patty," I said, "the thing is you did it. It doesn't come naturally to you, but if you keep doing it, you, me—anyone— can learn a new behavior."

Time and time again, putting shy people in social situations has proven to be one of the most effective tools I have encountered for developing talent from within our organization. That is why I am such a fiend on drawing people out. I may never have seen a glint of sociability in them, but still, I make the effort, and every once in a while I unleash a dynamo.

One of the discoveries of which I am proudest is our head of market research, Maria Koukotas. If you had met Maria when she first started with us, you would never in a million and half years have picked her as a potentially dynamic professional. "Quiet as a churchmouse" would have been too boisterous a description for Maria.

Then, one night after a particularly draining Mother's Day rush, we threw one of our international parties— gigantic pot-luck dinners. Our work force is rather ethnically diverse. Someone always brings Jamaican jerked chicken, a bathtub-size portion of lasagna with fresh Italian sausages, tacos with manhood-testing doses of chile peppers. There's music and inevitably some dancing in the aisles.

International Night serves a lot of purposes. It's an excuse to have some fun at work. By now you know that fun is the one thing that I always strive to inject into any situation. International Night is a chance for the company to do something for the staff—again, an activity that always pays dividends. And it gives me a chance to mix with, meet, and interact with people who are on the front lines of the company and, because of that, not in regular contact with the boss.

I had seen Maria around but had never exchanged more than a casual hello with her. Then, at this particular post–Mother's Day bash, Maria brought a tray of those unbelievably sweet, buttery, nutty pastries called baklava. In between licking the honey off my fingers and swallowing gulps of hot, thick Greek coffee, I struck up a conversation with Maria. She was very quiet, but there was something winning about her smile and the gracious way she took a compliment.

We continued to talk. I learned that she was a single mom (her husband had died a few years before). She had a daughter the same age as mine, which opened the conversational doors. When it came to her daughter, Tina, shy and retiring Maria was savvy, smart, and downright gabby. "This gal is a buried live wire," I said to myself, and made a note to mark her for special attention from our marketing manager.

"Keep an eye on Maria. There's more there than meets the eye," I advised. "Give her more responsibilities and see how she responds."

That's all Maria needed. Once she found that we had confidence in her, that gave her confidence in herself, and she and I had a special relationship. We would talk about our daughters, and I would always beg for more pastry. She and I had a direct "contact," and this, in turn, helped build her confidence further. Maria eagerly took each new assignment. We put her into a demanding market research project, and immediately she demonstrated great insight and analytical capabilities.

Maria is now our head of market research, and I am very grateful for my sweet tooth as a management recruiting tool!

## CALL ME OPRAH

Once or twice a year we throw a big party, inviting new hires and senior management. The expectation at these events is that I will get up and give a rah-rah speech to rally the troops for an even bigger year. Listening to the Beloved Founder jabber on about what a great company we have and how we are all in the same boat is one of the most surefire ways of putting a crowd to sleep.

Instead, I turn the tables on the crowd and ask them to talk. I walk around the room like Phil Donahue or Oprah, carrying a handheld mike, and I ask people at random to talk about the job, the company, something that happened over Christmas, a satisfying call from a customer, how we could do things more efficiently.

You can see the fear in people's eyes as I stalk the room. Nobody knows what I am going to ask next, and nobody wants to be the guinea pig. One year I noticed Elizabeth Kick, one of our BloomNet managers, watching me approach. She gave an absolutely magnificent performance as a nervous wreck, begging me in every nonverbal way not to call on her. It flashed through my mind that a heart attack was not out of the question.

The meeting went off well. People told war stories of

their first Christmas rush. We picked up a few good ideas, and I got a sense of the personalities of a lot of our new people. I counted it as a successful night, until Elizabeth came up to me looking on the verge of tears.

"Elizabeth, what's happened? You look so upset," I said out of genuine concern.

"I am really bothered that you didn't call on me," she said. It was the last thing I expected to hear.

"Elizabeth, I really thought there was every possibility you would die of embarassment if I did."

"I was just thinking about what I was going to say, and, yeah, I was nervous, but I finally figured if everyone else could do it, why not give it a shot?"

Before the room cleared, I took the mike and said, "I really want to apologize. I left out somebody who wanted to share her thoughts with us."

I gave the microphone to Elizabeth, who talked for ten minutes about how important our work was, how it helped people connect with family, friends, and loved ones at important times. She told a few anecdotes about people with whom she had spoken in recent months. Elizabeth wasn't the most polished speaker, but there was a believable and introspective quality that rang true.

I recruited Elizabeth into my traveling team, a group of our people whom I ask to work the room whenever we are called on to give a big presentation. I will station our folks at the entrances, where they will greet people, help certain key members of the audience to their seats, chat with them, make them feel at home. After the talk, there are inevitably more people wanting to ask me questions than

I can get to. So I point out our people to the crowd and let everyone know that they will be on hand to answer questions. Now, instead of ten or twenty encounters after a speech, we have fifty or even a hundred and fifty. We have started business relationships that way, found new hires, picked up terrific ideas that are moneymakers. Once again, my mantra of "make contact . . . make contact . . . make contact" serves us well. Furthermore, we have begun to develop a second tier of speakers. Instead of needing to book Jim McCann, our brand is now strong enough that "A Speaker from 1-800-FLOWERS" is a worthwhile event. The growth in contacts has been exponential.

Elizabeth Kick is now one of our presenters. Where she originally got by on just heart and soul, she now has added polish and warmth to her presentations.

## Seven Rules Of Pretty Good Speech-Giving

Here's how I give a speech. My rules aren't hard-and-fast. They follow no particular system but are the result of trial and error and a lot of advice from people whose presentation styles I admire.

- **Don't Talk to the Audience.** There is an expression to describe a crowd: "a faceless mass." You can't talk to a faceless mass. You can't tell it a joke or make it cry. You need to personalize any crowd. Pick out two or three people and talk to them. Keep coming back to them. Gauge their responses to your jokes, your killer stories, your emotion-rousing anecdotes.

- *No Windshield Wipers.* "Stare into the middle distance; move your head back and forth as if you are watching a tennis match." This is the advice some blockhead recommended in Public Speaking 101, and nobody bothered to drop the advice from subsequent editions. Instead, focus on a few sets of eyeballs. They will be the best test of how well you are doing.

- *Talk to Women.* Most speakers I know, or at least most male speakers, try to make contact with men in the audience. Big mistake. Guys guard their emotions. I always pick a few women with whom to make eye contact. I feel I get a truer emotional read. Of course, this could have something to do with communication between the sexes. Maybe women speakers find that guys are a better test of contact. But as a rule, there are fewer stonefaces among women than among men.

- *Have A Semi-Plan, Not a Prepared Text.* Unless you're giving a legal deposition, don't try to plan every word. Your speech will inevitably sound canned. Make a list of a dozen or so points you need to make. There's no law that you have to get through all of them. In the best of all possible worlds, people are going to remember one or two things. Never try to give a word-for-word speech. Pick three points you absolutely have to hit. Then play the rest by ear. If the audience isn't responding to a point, move on to the next. Don't give a college lecture. No one is going to be tested on what you say. Nine times out of ten your objective is to come across as a good guy from an interesting company.

- *Attack All Bozos.* Ill-mannered people are like dogs who keep jumping up on your leg. If you don't knock them down, they will keep on doing it. If a few people are giving me a hard time during a speech by making noise or carrying on side conversations, I will look them right in the eye. I will walk toward them, lean over to them, and make no bones about confronting them. As a speaker, I have a tremendous weapon: I can embarrass the living daylights out of them. And I let them know in every nonverbal way at my command that "I am watching you, and as long as you keep this up I am going to keep coming back to you." I will give the offender a few seconds to let my glare sink in, then turn back to him as if to say, "Good. We have an agreement. I will move away, but I will be back in a few seconds to make sure we still have an agreement." This may sound a little aggressive, but I realized early on that it was a necessary technique. If you lose the crowd, why give the speech?

- *Mistakes Don't Hurt.* In an episode of one of Julia Child's cooking shows, she's preparing a big family dinner. She's at the point of putting a stuffed turkey into the oven when everything slipped to the floor. Rather than tossing it out, Julia picked the bird up, put it back in the pan, and popped it into the oven. Turning to the camera Julia said, "Remember, we are alone in the kitchen." There is a great lesson to take from Julia. You may forget a point, stumble over a word, backtrack in your development of a point, but if you don't draw attention to it, if you don't get that guilty "oops" look in your eye, it's going to fly right by your audience. A little gaffe here and there lets them know that your speech is happening at the moment and not being delivered by rote.

- *The Sound of Silence.* Once you get over your fear of mistakes, you may discover that another one of your fears—the fear of sudden silence—can be your ally. A good presentation is like a house built of bricks. It's the placement of and the spaces between the bricks that give interest, definition, and emphasis to the architecture. Don't be afraid to take a moment to look at your notes, to scan the room after you make a big point, to collect your thoughts. This is known as a dramatic pause. To the speaker, it may seem very long, but to the audience, it's an effective element of a well-crafted speech. Remember that silence can work in your favor. Don't rush to get everything said. Stop for a second and make eye contact. It is often the pause that refreshes.

# MINING YOUR GREATEST RESOURCE: YOUR WORKFORCE

If shyness is the great inhibitor of people, the ability to communicate is the great liberator: It releases creativity, creates community, and subjects old ways of doing things to healthy public criticism. It is all part and parcel of my core belief that enhancing connections and keeping the information constantly flowing has an exponential effect on the ability of the organization to generate new ideas, respond to crises, and move forward as one. The bonus when you liberate shy people in this way is that they have been holding a lot in for a long time. When they start to plug in and contribute, you will often find that the dynamic go-getter that you have been looking for has been laboring quietly in Marketing or Customer Service or Operations all these years.

The shyness apple doesn't fall far from the tree. At least it didn't for my daughter, Erin. In my case, working with the public at Dadson's clothing store helped draw me out and develop the people skills I never knew I had. Erin's was a different story. I had encouraged her, as I have all my kids, to get a job in a service business where working for tips would help her learn how to interact with people. To describe her as a bundle of nerves—and shy nerves at that—doesn't begin to tell the story. But after a month when nobody had bitten off her ear, she began to feel comfortable at work. Shortly after that, a friend of hers needed someone to cover for her at another local restaurant. Erin volunteered to help out, this time with more self-assurance. She fit right in with the crowd, joking and joshing with the best of them. Without her shyness holding her back, she was able to look around at the business, and that's where some innate business savvy came out. Erin noticed that about a third of of all the checks had a mistake. So she did what any Cyber-Age kid would do: She got on her trusty laptop computer and did some calculations.

The next day, my "shy" daughter, who supposedly knew nothing about business, went up to the owner of the café and said, "You need to computerize." Without waiting for the owner to ask "When did you become an expert on my business?" Erin whipped out her spreadsheet and said, "Look, I did some calculations. Out of any twenty checks I picked, seven had a miscalculation. Say half of those mistakes are not in your favor. You're losing money. If half are in your favor, you are cheating your customers. That can really hurt your business in a hurry."

Now comes the part that really made me proud. As Erin tells it, she leaned forward like an insurance salesperson about to close a deal. "If my figures are projectable, you can't afford *not* to buy a computer. In fact, if these numbers hold up, I project that the computer will pay for itself in ninety days." A cost-benefit analysis from my shrinking-violet teenage daughter! Get rid of the shyness, and the inner talents flow. It happens every time.

## Chapter Fourteen

# Core Players and Hired Guns

Although I am always telling people not to dwell on mistakes, it is also human nature that there are some things that we just can't help revisiting, trying to figure out how we could have done things differently. Ralph Branca surely would not have thrown Bobby Thompson that pitch. Steve Jobs would not have hired John Scully. David Caruso wouldn't have left *NYPD Blue*. 1-800 FLOWERS would have held on to Tim.

Tim was a bright and extremely talented young manager who I expected to be with the company forever. I thought our future and his were linked. Then Tim got engaged. His wife-to-be had a different view of companies. In her book, a small entrepreneurial company like ours had neither the cachet nor the security of a big, name-brand *Fortune* 500 company. One of her brothers worked for Bear Stearns, another for American Express.

"How can I tell my friends and relatives that my husband works for some flower company?" she would ask as if every sane person in the world would agree that staying with us would be career suicide.

Tim had a problem. How could he stick with a job when the girl he was going to marry would always see him as an also-ran and small-timer? Like the folks in my old neighborhood who advised me to become a cop or work for Con Edison, Tim's bride had a slightly more upscale but similar view: Security and advancement lay with the tried-and-true companies.

Tim's work suffered. Although I was the one who eventually had to let him go, Tim had in effect quit mentally and spiritually as his fiancée's constant harping on our pipsqueak status took its toll. It became impossible to continue, so I called it quits.

As things turned out, Tim and his wife didn't see the way the corporate world was going. The tried-and-true brands of fifteen years ago have had a rough go of it. The true engine of wealth and growth has come from the former upstarts, the entrepreneurs. We, the entrepreneurs, were the horse to back. We have not had to downsize. Others have.

And Tim? I hope he's doing well.

That experience stayed with me. On the one hand, it taught me that there are people who are going to move on and that your obligation to them (and the way to attract them in the first place) is to increase the value of your brand.

On the other hand, it also taught me that there are people whom I see as core people: employees to whom I am bound by ties of loyalty, common experience, and mutual trust. They are the long-term heart of the company. They will always have a job as long as I have one. At the same time, and I have seen this more and more in recent years, there are specialized hired guns whom you absolutely must call in from time to time. They get paid more, they are higher maintenance, but you need them.

# DESIGNING MEN

People buy flowers because they are pretty. They buy from one florist rather than another because the arrangements are pretty. The people who do the best arranging are often extremely artistic types. They can sometimes be demanding and self-centered, but who are you going to hire to design your arrangements? Your accountant? Very early on I learned that you can't have the same expectations of every employee, you can't treat them all the same, and you can't pay them by similar criteria.

Take Bob Royce. This guy is one of the greatest designers I have come across. I have often thought that if God or Mother Nature were taking a walk among his arrangements, they would pause and say, "That's how I meant to do it. I'll make a note for the next time."

Bob is also high maintenance. He'll show up for two months and then, tiring of us, head across town to some expensive shop in Manhattan. I'll ask him to do a display for

$500 at a trade show and he'll come in at $1,250. Come to think of it, I don't give him a price anymore because it is totally irrelevant to him and I always like his work. Woe to me, however, if I don't fall down on the floor, clutch my chest, and shout with glee when he shows me his work. Bob needs reinforcement like a tapeworm needs tape (or whatever it is that tapeworms need). Invariably, Bob eventually feels underappreciated and he takes a walk until the next time I need him.

Although professional football is not the first analogy that comes to mind when dealing with Bob, I eventually realized a great similarity between the Bobs of this world and the Dallas Cowboys' cornerback Deion Sanders. Sanders, like Bob, is a high-strung player. And like Bob he is creative and comes through in high-stakes situations. When Dallas Cowboy owner Jerry Jones wanted a Super Bowl a few seasons back, he felt that it was worth any price to lure the best cornerback in the world away from the San Francisco 49ers.

There are people like Sanders or Bob—I call them "Neon Deions"—who are uniquely qualified to fulfill an immediate need. You need them and they want the paycheck so you hire them. It's all a matter of matching skill sets to needs. This is fine when you are calling someone in for a defined short-term job, but, as in all things in business, it's never that cut-and-dried.

# YOU'RE GREAT, MEET YOUR NEW BOSS

Our company has always been known for its use of technology, and we've had a number of talented people in our IT (information technology) department. As the company has grown, though, so have our talent needs, and last year we decided that we needed to bring in an outsider to properly position our technology group for the twenty-first century.

Naturally, this wasn't the most popular decision among some of the people we already had on our IT team, and a couple of them left to pursue opportunities elsewhere. But most of the technology team, I'm proud to say, realized that working for Guru Ghosh (yes, we actually have a "guru" in charge of our technology) would add to their skill sets and ultimately make them more valuable to any employer.

Clearly, this kind of situation calls for delicate handling. And it is a situation that growing companies come across all the time. There comes a point when you have to bring in outside talent and bypass some of the staff that have been with you for some time. It's never easy, but you find out quickly who your core team players are.

Now, a year after Guru joined the company, our IT team is stronger than it's ever been. The whole department, from top to bottom. Which is what we hoped to accomplish in the first place.

# THE EAGLE HAS LANDED

It doesn't take a lot of inner fortitude to remain loyal to great employees—good producers, easy to get along with, all-around good people. You won't get any medals for that. But there aren't too many employees who fit that bill. The real test is when you stand by your people in spite of their imperfections—which sometimes can be pretty imperfect. Take the case of Lois and the eagle.

Lois was the cleaning lady in our old office in Bayside. She was the nicest person, able to cheer anybody up when they were down, and she took a personal interest in everybody at our office. She brought good vibes into the place, and I don't know how to put a number next to that on our balance sheet, though I know it was worth lots. Only problem was, Lois started out as a not-so-great cleaning lady and proceeded to get worse. She was the kind of cleaning lady that you had to clean up after.

I have a pretty simple office. Something about my Irish city kid background can't deal with mega-power offices. If someone gave me one, I would keep looking around waiting for the important person who "really deserved it" to come in. However I did have one expensive item in my old office, a beautiful Steuben glass eagle that was a gift from Jim Poage, who was my Dallas-based partner when I first bought 1-800-FLOWERS. It meant a lot to me, because my friendship with Jim meant a lot. By putting his money on the line with mine to back my vision, he helped make 1-800-FLOWERS go. And then he did something else extraordinary in business.

He knew when to bow out. After several months of my flying back and forth to Dallas to run the company, Jim had the character and good sense to see that I really didn't need him in the deal, and I sure didn't need to be schlepping down to Dallas as part of my regular commute. One night over a Chinese dinner, Jim and I had a heart to heart. "The big fires are out," he said. "The business is skinnied down to next to nothing. It really needs to be rebirthed. You're the entrepreneur. Why don't you buy me out and let me tend to my business issues here and you go back to New York and re-create the company?"

I already had a telemarketing operation in Queens, so I had the necessary infrastructure. When I took Jim up on his offer, the eagle was his gift to me. I never priced it, but having seen other Steuben pieces, I would guess it was a gift that cost some thousands of dollars.

One Sunday morning, our office manager, Leah, called me up at home shortly after Lois the cleaning lady had come in for a few hours, got her paycheck, and left.

"Jim," Leah said with a tense tone in her voice, "I don't know how to tell you this, but I have good news and bad news."

"What's the good news?" I asked.

"You know that eagle that Jim Poage gave you? Well, it seems Lois took it into her head to dust off your shelves"—something, by the way, that I had never known her to do before—"and she was on her tiptoes dusting the eagle when it crashed to the floor. The good news is, the eagle has landed."

"And the bad news, Leah?"

"The bad news is, he landed on his face!"

My beautiful eagle gone! Venus de Milo may look good without any arms, but an eagle without a head looks like a fresh-killed chicken.

Like I said, loyalty to great employees is a no-brainer. Putting up with the frailties of the rest of us takes some more patience.

## THE DOES-ALL LADY

A true core person doesn't know from job descriptions. All he or she knows is that the job has to get done. This is always true in any business, but as you get bigger and bigger and the company gets more compartmentalized the true Jack- (or Jill)-of-all-trades is harder to recognize. In the beginning, though, you ain't goin' nowhere without these kinds of people. This was driven home to me shortly after I had accepted Jim Poage's offer and decided to move the operation north.

It's one thing to say "I can do this; after all, I already have a telemarketing operation." It's quite another thing to have looked at the reality of one bank of telephones in our Bayside store. If our Flora Plenty telephone operation was going to become 1-800-FLOWERS, we needed more phones and places to put the people who worked the phones. At least, we had to hope we would need them.

One afternoon, my brother Chris and I hunkered down with a yellow pad as we wolfed down some franks and beans at a backyard barbecue. Chris roughed out a plan to pack a hundred pounds of telephone operation into our twenty-pound bag. I took the plan to Marge Duffy, one of our original employees from the "bucket shop" in the subway station. Marge, at that time, was in charge of the telecenter. She had also been head retail instruction person, payroll supervisor, and head of technical support.

Chris and I outlined the whole big new beautiful design for the upsized 1-800-FLOWERS telecenter, and Marge was brimming with enthusiasm. I remember her motioning to Joan Abruzzino, another longtime core player, and the two of them fell into a deep chat about our drawing.

The next morning Marge and Joan show up without their briefcases and wearing their rattiest jeans and sweatshirts. Marge had this big metal box, which she plunked down on the floor and opened. Out came a fierce-looking device called a Saws All, a huge rip toothed power saw used to take down studs and walls. She fired it up and began to dismantle our telecenter, with Joan right by her side. Chris and I got the message. Marge, whose husband was a gifted woodworker, knew all about every aspect of small-time construction. And she knew that Chris and I had grown up in the business. We weren't going to bid things out and wait for the contractors. We were going to do it ourselves. And Joan? No special construction skills, but Marge's can-do attitude was infectious. Within six days we had twenty-four work stations and, an even greater miracle, we basically had no down time on our telephone answering capability.

You may never know the reservoir of hidden talents in any organization. But if you give people the chance, they will often surprise you.

## YOU CAN'T HIRE THEM AND YOU CAN'T FIRE THEM

If I am an accidental entrepreneur, Bea is an accidental core person. When Bea first came to us back in the days when there were just a few flower shops, she had just retired from the Federal Reserve after thirty-five years. Her very rusty office skills were with a rotary phone, a manual typewriter, and a primitive adding machine on which you punched in the numbers and then pulled down a metal arm to make it go *ca-ching*. This was a set of skills right out of a romantic comedy set in an office in the 1940s.

But Bea had spirit, gallons of it. After her interview with Marge Duffy, our office manager, we were kind of 50-50 about hiring her. Bea didn't give us the chance to decide. Next day, when Marge arrived at work, Bea had beaten her there and even had a makeshift vase of flowers on a desk she had commandeered. She had set up an orange juice can as a pencil holder, and she was busy putting some call sheets in order.

Marge was a little bit taken aback by all this, so she said the first thing that came to her mind, a very practical "What are you doing here?"

"I couldn't wait to hear from you, so I just decided to come in and get myself started."

She was so nice and so eager that Marge didn't have the guts to tell her she wasn't on our payroll. Today, after ten years of service, Bea is one of our senior employees. And while she's not reinventing the accounting profession, there would be a great big emotional hole in that department if she weren't there. Her contribution is not bottom-line quantifiable, but it is undeniably tangible as it contributes to the spirit and morale of the company.

You may add to Bea's many valuable qualities the fact that she isn't a weenie. Every company needs someone whose guts and perseverance can be used to shame the fainthearted. I just never expected our profile in courage to come from a seventy-eight-year-old woman!

Two winters ago, we had twenty snowstorms in our area. Maybe it would be more accurate to say that we had one long snowstorm broken up by a few days when it didn't snow. The day before one of the biggies, the forecasters were having a field day, whipping all of Long Island into a blizzard frenzy. Of course it had to happen during the Valentine's rush, which I took as a sign of divine displeasure.

Anyway, the forecasters were wrong. Instead of ten inches we had the biggest snowstorm of the year. As a kid I can remember snow that came up to my thighs, but that was when I was about two-foot-six. Both me and my thighs are somewhat taller now. So was the snow.

Chris and I both have four-wheel drives, so we were able to make it to work along with nine other people (a normal shift that time of year is about 200-plus). So we all started answering phones. A number of customers said I sounded just like Jim McCann on the commercials, and they didn't really believe me when I said I was (I guess it would be kind of like having Michael Eisner meeting you for a tour of Disney World).

Just about that time Bea walked in. She was so bundled

up in scarves, wool hat, galoshes, and other implements of weather protection that she looked like a cross between a bag lady and a small running back.

"Bea?" I said, shaking my head in semidisbelief. "You don't even work on this shift. You're a night person. What are you doing here?"

"Well, I saw the storm, and figured you would be short-handed. I didn't know how long it would take to get this place running, so I left my house at 4:30 and shoveled the car out, but the car wouldn't budge. So I walked to the bus, caught that to the train and, since there were no taxis, walked from there to here. It was only a couple of miles," she told me while her galoshes dripped pools of water on the floor.

Just then, one of my high-priced, hired-gun "Neon Deion" executives called me from the nearby hotel where we had put up some key people in anticipation of the storm.

"Jim, it's snowing like a son of a bitch," he said. "I don't know if I can get in to the office. There are no cars on the street and I don't think I can make it on foot."

I said, "Listen, Mr. Senior Management, I have a four-foot-ten, seventy-eight-year-old grandmother who just walked two miles into the teeth of the wind. Get your ass down here!"

Many other companies would have retired a person of Bea's age, but sometimes you have to look into your heart and ask yourself, "What will that person's spirit contribute to my company?" Bea's contributions are numerous, and I can't imagine our company without her.

## Chapter Fifteen

# Can't Buy Me Love

## ANOTHER KIND OF CURRENCY

When I was a kid you got paid by the hour, probably in cash, once a week. When you became a grown-up, you graduated to a weekly paycheck. Those seemed to be the only two ways a human received compensation in my neighborhood. Then I started a company and the company grew. All of a sudden our people—the kind of highly skilled career management people that we have needed more and more—were interested in more than their paycheck. They talked about a "compensation package." What benefits was I offering, how much vacation, stock options, bonuses? Business life, it turns out, is a lot more than simply "You work, I pay."

There are consultants who will tell you how to craft a compensation package that will stay in line with your overall structure and still remain competitive within your industry. But there is a whole other compensation package that I have worked on since my days at St. John's: emotional compensation.

Every job is going to pay you money. You don't go to work for the hugs. But money isn't the only form of gratification that a work relationship can offer. Emotional connections, a whole range of them, will bind people to your company and to each other. It is only when you have that kind of bonding that a group of salaried employees becomes an entity that is greater than the sum of its parts.

You might say that this lesson hit me over the head. Or better, it didn't hit me over the head . . . Thank God.

## DUCK!!

When I first started at the group home, I was casting around blind. As Brother Tom pointed out, I didn't have a program. I was trying to establish some kind of relationship with the boys. There was one, Elwin Jones, who seemed like he wasn't too far from getting back into the mainstream of life. Elwin went to Beach Channel High in the Rockaways, which was a long train ride from the group home. He was a terrific football player, not very big, but, like Emmit Smith or Rodney Hampton, he was compact and powerful. He was a valuable member of the team and its only African American. He was also the only kid on the team who had no family members coming out and rooting for him. It wasn't because his family wasn't interested. He had no family. This kid was alone.

I became his rooting section. I offered to go out to the games with him, but he didn't want me coming along—I might look like a parole officer or caseworker. No, I had to show up in the stands the way a family member or a friend would. Elwin, who did so-so in school, had all the right work habits when it came to football: he showed up at practice, he studied, he worked hard. After I went out to see him in a few games, Elwin started to look for me in the stands. I would be there yelling, "Way to go, Elwin!"

We became pals. This was a kid who had never had anyone in his corner. And then one day he showed up in mine. I probably had not been at the group home more than a few months and was still very much feeling my way into how to reach the boys. One of them, Raymond, was a real tough dude. Worse, he would fly into a rage over nothing.

One night we were watching a ball game. Raymond got royally teed off that he wasn't going to see his favorite sitcom because we were watching the Mets. He went haywire. I was in a high-backed chair and Elwin was sitting on the couch as we watched Cleon Jones try to bring the Mets back in the late innings. Suddenly, out of the corner of my eye, I registered an odd sight: Raymond, coming straight at me, with a baseball bat.

Just as he swung the bat I flew out of the chair and hit the floor. CRASSHH! The chair exploded in smithereens as Raymond came down on it with the bat. He began to reload for another swing. I remember seeing a wild, mad dog look in his eyes and thinking, "That's it, Jim, this is where the story ends." I tried to get to my feet to get out of the way, but Raymond was faster than I was. This was going to be really bad.

Then Elwin was coming—he leapt off the couch and, as Raymond was at the apex of his windup, Elwin ripped into his side with a tackle that drove him into the wall. By then I was able to get to my feet and assist Elwin in subduing Raymond.

When I calmed down that night, I reflected on what had happened. It struck me that in some sense Elwin felt indebted to me. It wasn't a money thing, but it was nonetheless a debt. My going to those games had been an investment in our relationship. I was hoping that my return on investment would be a motivated kid doing better in school. I got that, and I also got someone who saved my life.

That episode stirred something in me. I still needed to give it a form.

## DON'T LEAVE (THE ST. JOHN'S HOME) WITHOUT IT

What I gave Elwin was recognition. It was one of the few currencies that we could be free with at St. John's. We certainly didn't have the green kind to spread around. It was just after the Raymond incident that I began to spend time with Les Goldberg, Dr. Dick Scalon, and Jim Vitale. Les, who is now the head of government affairs at American Express, is a great motivator; he has applied the experience with the kids at St. John's to a workforce of forty thousand at

AmEx. Dick Scalon was, and still is, a very perceptive, accomplished, and caring psychologist. Jim is now teaching school in Brooklyn.

They worked out a "compensation package" at St. John's that was at the core of every success story there. Our goal, plain and simple, was behavior modification. Our weapons were positive reinforcement. It wasn't that we didn't believe in negative reinforcement (which, by the way, I don't); it was just that we were discouraged strenuously from ever resorting to punishment.

Their compensation package dealt in three currencies: recognition, status, and money. We created five levels that you could achieve. Each level had responsibilities and rewards: more lenient curfew, a trip to the Yankee game, a bigger allowance, the chance to set your own study hours, your own room. As people took more responsibility, the rewards gave them more independence, requiring more responsibility. Of course, the end goal was having the boys being able to take responsibility for themselves.

The boys, for the most part, responded beautifully. They wanted the perks that went with moving up the ladder but, interestingly, these five levels that we made up took on a life of their own. The ranks became a tangible, sought-after commodity. In other words, if you create a hierarchy, if you create different classifications of people, it is in our nature to want to rise in that context. And furthermore, the act of social recognition was one more currency added into a total compensation package that had very little to do with money. It had to do with privileges and responsibilities and being singled out for special attention.

At 1-800-FLOWERS we never cease trying to find ways to recognize people and their contribution with more than money—although I have yet to come across the employee who says "no thanks" to a raise. Theater tickets, plane rides, dinner with the spouse at a great restaurant, ethnic nights that celebrate the different nationalities working for us, a chance to speak on behalf of the company—all these things that I have talked about over and over in this book share one common element: They connect personally with our employees. They send the message: "You are appreciated and you are special."

You cannot overdo recognition. You cannot overpraise. They are inexhaustible resources that cost nothing and buy you more goodwill among your employees than anything else you can do. If you establish this pattern early on, then it becomes one of the tools in your kit that can allow you to deal with the ever-present question of monetary compensation.

## CORPORATE NONCOMS

An army in the field could get along a lot more easily without lieutenants than without sergeants. There are people who were born to be sergeants, who do it better than anyone else, who have an ability to deal with the stress and strain of life on the front lines. Put that same person in the officer corps and he or she doesn't function the same way. "Fish out of water" is the phrase that comes to mind.

As I explained previously, we have been able to work our way through bringing high-ticket specialists in at a higher salary than some of the people who have been with us for years. Special talents get special rates. In part, the fact that these specialists came from the outside helped: there wasn't a history with these people so they weren't busting out of the same salary structure that everyone else worked under. If people could be seen as cars, then these new employees were high-priced options. Unlike the core team members, though, these high-priced options are not kept beyond the period of your specific need.

But recently, when thinking over the big picture of 1-800-FLOWERS, I reflected that the true heart and soul of the company, the engine that drives everything else, is the telerep. That person who can connect one-on-one with the customer is where the magic happens. The most successful reps have an innate ability to make contact. By and large, they are not born managers. On more than one occasion when we have promoted a great rep to manager, we lost a great rep and gained a not-so-great manager. I am reminded of something that a former *National Lampoon* editor once said when asked about comedy writers: "There are probably fifty people in America who can truly write comedy. If you find one, treat him like gold."

Like comedy writers, or quarterbacks, or great composers, or salespeople, there is just so much great telerep DNA to go around. I was in a quandary. My best people all wanted to be supervisors so that they could move up the title hierarchy and get paid more. I thought about this for a while, then I realized that not every title has to convey a sense of the reporting relationship in a company. Some titles can be outside the hierarchy. In the church there are priests, monsignors, bishops, cardinals, the Pope, and his Boss. And then there are saints. They don't fit into the hierarchical structure in any way, but they, too, are the heart and soul of the enterprise.

We came up with the notion of master reps. We pay master reps more than other reps and, often, more than supervisors. This was a complete win situation. The reps stayed where they could do the most good for the company. They really glowed with the special recognition they got in the new master category. We made a big deal about them in our internal communications, plastered their pictures on our walls, and treated them like stars. Their supervisors were happy because their people were meeting sales projections. And if all those people are happy, then, as a cultural engineer, I'm happy too.

You may say that the only currency I was dealing with here was money, and while it is true that money definitely entered into the equation, it is equally true that the non-monetary aspects of this event—the twin currencies of recognition and status—enabled us to establish new compensation levels while maintaining harmony in our workforce.

## AND THE EMPLOYEE OF THE MONTH IS SOMEONE WHO DOESN'T WORK FOR US . . .

Recognition, contact, challenging work—they are all part and parcel of the overarching theme of everything I do, in business and outside of it: namely, to establish connection and the free flow of energy among people. Open up those emotional pipes and you succeed. Close them and you become an isolated manager in an isolated company that the world will sooner or later pass by.

And don't confine your recognition to your employees. Find a way to recognize your customers. I realized the importance of this tool a couple of years ago when I was chewing the fat with a few of our florists and we got to the issue of charity. Now, if you have ever been to a charity dinner or luncheon, you probably recall that every table had a floral centerpiece. What you may not know is that in every town where there is a florist, you can be sure that there is a charity that has asked for free flowers.

They are all worthy causes, but we can't give flowers away to these events any more than a caterer can give away the food. We would literally go out of business. Still, we want to help, and we hit upon an idea that works unbelievably well for everybody involved.

Say you are the chairperson for the annual dinner for the heart association. You approach 1-800-FLOWERS for a donation. Well, we won't donate the flowers, but we can save you a lot of money on arrangements. If you bring a dozen people from your organization down to our shop, we will have some of our designers on hand, and we will donate our workspace, tools, and personnel to help you make up your centerpieces.

So on the afternoon of your event, you come with a bunch of people from your group and we sit around for a couple of hours, working together, putting together arrangements that end up costing you much less than you would have paid for us to design and make them up. Then you go to your banquet, and everything looks great. You feel especially good about the flowers because you made them. At the end of the meal, the master of ceremonies gives a little thank-you to 1-800-FLOWERS and our company's guy or gal comes to the podium with a big envelope and says something like the following:

> We're really happy that 1-800-FLOWERS could be part of this event, but I have to tell you, this terrific work wasn't a result of our putting our best designers on the job. In fact, tonight's arrangements were done by a team of rookies who had never done anything like this before. So I would like to hand out some plaques and certificates to recognize this group.

At that point we start to read off the names of the people from the charity who came down to help us and we have a photographer there to take pictures. The end result is that the event went well, the flowers were great, and we now have ten disciples who have been in our shop, got to know our people well, and whom we have publicly recognized. Contact, fun, recognition, connection. It's not cash, but it is the currency that fills the bank accounts in the contact economy.

## Chapter Sixteen

# We Interrupt This Broadcast . . .

## TOLSTOY WAS DEAD WRONG

When I was in college, I took World Lit 101, and among the books we had to read was *Anna Karenina* by Leo Tolstoy. We had a few choices, but I went with Anna because the back cover said it had to do with adultery and I was an eighteen-year-old boy, so I hoped for some hot parts. I have two things to report. Although it is a terrific story, there are no hot parts. And secondly, I urge you to consider the opening lines. "All happy families are the same, each unhappy family has a different tale to tell."

That may be true for families, but not so for business. In my experience, all unhappy businesses are the same: they go out of business. But every successful business is a thing unto itself. If I hadn't seen an ad for a flower franchise while wolfing down a baloney sandwich one afternoon in Queens, I might today be the proud operator of a carwash on Lefferts Boulevard, or maybe a McDonalds somewhere on Long Island. A lot of things had to happen just right before my desire to be a businessman turned into a successful enterprise. The original 1-800-FLOWERS guys in Dallas had run out of time with their big idea so they would need to unload the company. Bernie Lynch had to front me three months' worth of flowers because my cash flow was basically minus. And on and on. So, yes, there are lessons to draw from my experience, and I am not going to let you finish this book without laying my deeply considered wisdom on you (again). But before I do that, remember that businesses, like people, have lives. And life is a one-time event.

## WHY PEOPLE KNOW MY FACE

Although I would be hard-pressed to claim that I have memorable looks, people do recognize me. I rarely get through an airport without someone saying, "Hey, aren't you the flower guy?" In large measure, this recognition factor has to do with my appearing in our commercials. And in even larger measure it has to do with the commercials we ran on CNN during the Gulf War.

Shortly after we changed our company name to 1-800-FLOWERS we began to run spots on CNN. As TV time goes, it wasn't that expensive and it reached the right audience. Say you're a businessperson on the road watching

CNN while you get ready to go to dinner. Our commercial comes on. You remember a thank-you or a birthday. You see our number. You order flowers. If it happened one time, it happened ten thousand. The confluence of 800 technology, the rise of CNN, and my getting into the long-distance flower business all happened at the same time, and it all worked in our favor.

Add to that the fact that Ted Turner is my kind of businessman. He takes risks. He defies the common wisdom. He is very much his own man. When we first met at a conference years ago, I was extremely flattered when Ted sought me out and told me how much he liked the way our company was "kicking ass." That was the beginning of a mutually admiring and supportive relationship. CNN did so well for us that we kept buying more and more time.

Then the Gulf War happened. CNN's ratings went through the roof. That one-time event made it *the* global television news network. Anywhere you go, anywhere in the world, you are more likely to see CNN on in the background than any other network. When you enter the unbelievably high-tech network control center for AT&T there is an enormous wall of monitors with a large map indicating phone traffic that is currently being generated in the United States. Right smack dab in the middle of that wall is a big monitor playing CNN. The AT&T gurus figure if there is an earthquake, a stock market dip, a plane crash, hurricane, assassination, or World Series victory, it is going to indicate a big spike in demand on their network, and having just that few minutes of advance warning puts them on notice to have all backup systems fired up.

So, yes, the Gulf War was good for CNN's ratings, but not so good for its ad sales. Would you want to have your commercial for the Good Olds Guys full of happy families and weekend fun scheduled to run right before the pictures of our soldiers advancing in the dark desert on the outskirts of Kuwait City? Many advertisers, not wanting to seem uncaring or unpatriotic, pulled a lot of their frivolous good-times commercials, and CNN was left with a lot of eyeballs glued to their reporting as well as a huge unused inventory of commercial time.

Before I had the chance to consider pulling out of our time on CNN, one of Ted's people called me and basically said, "Look, we can understand a lot of the companies pulling out. The whole thing is very sensitive and no one wants to look like they're profiting on a national crisis. But people are very emotional in wartime. They need to express those emotions. Soldiers need to send flowers to their moms and wives and sweethearts. We think you would be doing the right thing to stay on the air. We just wanted to tell you that."

It made sense. I bought a lot of the newly available inventory on CNN. We had special deals for armed forces members and their families. Ted charged us the normal rates on CNN, which guaranteed something like a 1.0 rating, but with the whole world tuned in to Peter Arnett and those gripping pictures of Baghdad, CNN was getting ratings of 23 and 24—*Seinfeld* level. The number of impressions our business made was enormous. Ever since that time 1-800-FLOWERS has been perceived as a real brand name. As much as I would like to say that it was in the cards, and that my gung ho entrepreneurship would have made this happen eventually, I am not so sure that the story would have been the same without a push from that one-time event. Or, to put it another way, opportunity never announces in advance when it is going to come knocking. Make sure you're not hanging around in your underwear. Put some jeans on. Answer the door.

## Ten Semi-Commandments

So now that I have told you why every business is different and how success often has as much to do with the roll of the dice as the smarts of the entrepreneur, I would like to share my rules of success. Hear me out, then feel free to break them.

### Waste Your Youth in Higher Pursuits

The way I read most "How to Succeed" books, you need to be born with a U.S. Robotics Palm Pilot grafted onto your frontal lobe. You must live, breathe, and think business from earliest childhood. Stray from this path and your competitors will whiz by in a cloud of cyberdust.

I don't think so. My fourteen years at the St. John's Home for Boys taught me lessons that translated instantly to running a global business. Motivating, setting goals, managing crises: These were the daily tasks involved in getting a group of "at-risk" kids to jump-start their lives. I still use those same social work skills that I learned back then. In fact, the bigger my business has become, the more my job description looks like it did back in the Rockaways. I was and still am a cultural engineer, but the pay is a lot better for entrepreneurs than it is for social workers.

### Don't Go Crazy About Not Getting an MBA

Do I wish I had gone to Harvard Biz and could sling B-speak with the rest of them? You bet! Business school gives you a shorthand for thinking and communicating with all the other business school graduates. It gives you a vocabulary that is understood everywhere that business is done. It helps you analyze business situations. But, given the choice, I would much rather be a case study than read about one. Henry Ford didn't go to business school. Ted Turner didn't. Bill Gates didn't. Sometimes throwing yourself into the thick of business and seeing if you can swim is the best way. If you are a born entrepreneur—you will float.

### Don't Try to Know Everything Beforehand

There is no question in my mind: If I had known all about the flower business before I went into it, I probably would have saved my money and not bought that first franchise. And I surely would never have bought 1-800-FLOWERS. The simple fact of the matter is that you need to start down the road before you can see where it leads you. I didn't have to go into the flower business. I just needed something to do to put more food on the table. Flowers, fast food, a shoe store, a personal computer business in the garage—the skill set is the same for almost every business. If you have a sense of adventure and entrepreneurship, take that first step.

## Brand Yourself

In an era where careers and companies change so fast, I sometimes think, not totally in jest, "Gee, I remember when warp speed was fast!" Since very few of us can count on being at the same company or in the same business for all of our working life, the only real constant you can deal with and control is YOU. Treat yourself like a brand and remember consistency and credibility are the two greatest assets any brand can have. Sharpen your message, work on your image, and make sure you deliver. In that way you become a known quantity in a changing world.

## SOBs Finish Last

Okay, I'm lying. While it's true that there are a lot of ruthless types who make a success of themselves, I have found that it is just as true that building relationships with people was the only way that I was able to forge ahead. And as technology becomes more diffused and more companies are able to achieve the same quality of product, then the race will go to the nicest. Given a choice, folks will always choose to do business with people and companies that value them.

### Remember the Wheel Was Already Invented

It has been said that there are only six plots in the world and that all the books and plays are just variations on those themes. Business is the same. Enter every situation, every encounter, every meeting, every interview with the intention of learning something. Seen in this light, creativity becomes the ability to learn from others' experience and to apply those lessons in new situations. That's why I consider myself a creative plagiarist. If I am on the board of a company, I look to see how they do things. If someone wants to be one of my vendors, I want to know about their quality control, their compensation structure, their use of technology. In almost everything new that you attempt, someone has already done it, sometimes successfully and sometimes not. There is a lesson to learn either way.

### Cheap Is Cheap

It is a truism that the smart entrepreneur goes where the labor is cheapest. Wrong. Go where the labor is smartest. With labor, as with so much else in life, you get what you pay for. Maybe cheap labor doesn't matter all that much in some businesses, but it can be hell on a service business. When we moved 1-800-FLOWERS to Long Island, we immediately incurred some of the highest business costs in the nation and yet the company flourished as never before. Why? I think it has a lot to do with New Yorkers having developed the skill to get along with all types of people. We have Italians, African Americans, Greeks, Chinese, Mexicans, Irish, all living and working with one another. These are people who need extraordinary people skills in order to survive, and those are just the kinds of skills that you need to service a global clientele.

### Trust Those Family Ties

I was brought up in a family business that in some respects didn't work. My father and one of his brothers were often at each other's throats. On the other hand, my brother Chris and my two sisters have all played major roles in our company. (Come to think of it, so has my other brother, Kevin, from time to time.) The principle to bear in mind is that a dysfunctional family will probably have a dysfunctional family business. Mind you, I am not saying that there is no such thing as sibling rivalry or that it doesn't drive me crazy when my sister pulls our her emery board to work on a nail when we are talking (or that she doesn't wince when I do my bad imitation of the guys who used to work in Dad's business). We're all human and we all get under each other's skin some of the time. But in our free-agent, deal-based world, only family is forever.

### High Margins Aren't Always Important

Forget margins. Are you giving customers what they want, when they want it? Are you making it easier for them to do business with you? Are you creating a culture where employees feel appreciated and respected and where they are passing this feeling on to your public? Do you challenge, reinforce, and reward the people who work for you?

Take care of these "marginal" details and the margins will take care of themselves. And never rest on your laurels, because no matter how well you are doing this year, by the time next year rolls around, everyone will be aping your successes and you will have to do even better.

### Get Personal

I have heard it said that people who star in their own commercials have fools for talent. Yes—but . . .

The "but" comes in when you consider that a company like ours with a name like 1-800-FLOWERS didn't leap out of the box and give everybody a warm and fuzzy feeling. Buying flowers for someone is a personal act, so our customers had to see that we were a personal business. By appearing in our ads, I let people know that I am a real florist and this is a family business. It all gets back to the contact economy. If you can find a way to make contact, you are way ahead of the game. If it just so happens that a commercial is the way to do it—then do it.

### Special Bonus Commandment: Planless Isn't Clueless

Business plans are good for something, but not necessarily for starting a business. I know it wasn't true in our case. We started out with a small chain of retail shops. We built that into a very successful company. Then we became a 1-800 number, and that forced us to become a brand. Once we were telephonic, it was a logical jump into interactive. In the end our strategic business plan was "If it seemed like a good idea, we did it." Our business grew the way flowers do—organically.

# Chapter Seventeen

# In Conclusion

Today 740,000 people are celebrating their birthdays. To-morrow another 740,000 people will be celebrating theirs. If you'd like to make one or two of them feel terrific on their special day . . . I know a 1-800 number you can call.

## About the Author

JIM McCANN is president of 1-800-FLOWERS, the world's largest florist. Prior to becoming a florist more than twenty years ago, he was a social worker in New York City.

Jim regularly speaks to audiences around the world and was recently named Toastmasters International's top business speaker. He is also active in numerous business and community organizations, and serves on the boards of directors of Gateway 2000, OfficeMax, the National Retail Federation, PETCO Animal Supplies, and Very Special Arts. Jim lives on Long Island with his wife and three children.